Achievements of Civilization

THE BOOK OF WEALTH
Book Three

WEALTH IN RELATION TO MATERIAL

and

Intellectual Progress and Achievement

BEING

*An Inquiry into the Nature and Distribution of the World's
Resources and Riches, and a History of the Origin and Influence of
Property, its Possession, Accumulation, and Disposition in all Ages
and among all Nations,
as a Factor in Human Accomplishment, an Agency of Human
Refinement, and in the Evolution of Civilization
from the Earliest to the Present Era*

BY

HUBERT HOWE BANCROFT

NEW YORK

THE BANCROFT COMPANY, PUBLISHERS

1896

THE BOOK OF WEALTH was first published in 1896 by Hubert Howe Bancroft

This updated "Popular" edition published 2012 by BancroftBookofWealth.com

Prepared for publication by John R. Cumbow

THE BOOK OF WEALTH – Popular Edition – Book Three

ISBN-10: 1477559450
ISBN-13: 978-1477559451

www.BancroftBookofWealth.com

THE BOOK OF WEALTH – Popular Edition

Publisher's Note:

Originally published in 1896 in a special edition by Hubert Howe Bancroft, THE BOOK OF WEALTH consisted of 10 oversized volumes, bound in silk. The books were never intended for distribution to the general public. Only a few thousand copies were ever printed, and the books were marketed exclusively to the world's wealthiest families and individuals. Sold by subscription in strictly limited editions, the complete set was sold at that time for $2,500 — a very large sum of money even today!

More than 100 years old, the 10 volumes of THE BOOK OF WEALTH still offer valuable information for the modern reader. In order to make this rare set of books available to a wider audience, we are republishing the ten individual books in a modern 'Popular Edition' at a fraction of the original price.

Each of the books in our 'Popular Edition' includes the complete text from the original 'Fin de Siecle' edition published at the dawn of the 20th century. We've retained all of the original archaic language and spelling, as well as many of the engravings, line drawings and photogravures that illustrated the original volumes.

We trust that you, the modern reader, will find the contents of these rare books worthy of your attention.

www.BancroftBookofWealth.com

THE BOOK OF WEALTH

BOOK THREE

CONTENTS

CHAPTER THE SEVENTH

ITALY

Ergo sollicitae tu causa, pecunia, vitae es,
Per te immaturum mortis adimus iter.
Tu vitiis hominum crudelia pabula praebes;
Semina curarum de capite orta tuo.
— Propertius

Omnis enim res,
Virtus, fama, decus, divina humanaque,
pulchris Divitiis parent. *— Horace*

Creverunt et opes, et opum furiosa cupido;
Et cum possideant, plurima, plura volunt.
— Ovid

Non quare et unde; quid habeas tantum rogant. *— Seneca*

Avaritia et luxuria, quae pestes omnia magna imperia everterunt. *— Livy*

Nam divitiae, nomen, opes vacuae consilio et vivendi atque aliis imperandi modo, dedecoris plenae sunt et insolentis superbiae: nec ulla deformior species est civitatis, quam illa in qua opulentissimi optimi putantur. *— Tacitus*

O dii immortales! non intelligunt homines, quam magnum vectigal sit parsimonia. *— Cicero*

WHEN the first Greek colonists arrived in southern Italy, they found there peoples to whom they gave the name of Oenotrians, and Iapygians, or Messapians, both as it seems of Pelasgic or ancient Hellenic origin. It was probably to the territory of the former that the word Italia was first applied, its derivation being traced to the italoi, or oxen, for which that district was famous. Not until many centuries later was the term used to signify the entire peninsula. As colonies spread and prospered, the country south of the river Silarus became known as Magna Graecia; in the centre were various tribes and nations, chief among whom were the Etruscans, Umbrians, Sabines, Latins, Volscians, Aequians, and Oscans, while to the north were the Gauls, Ligurians, and Venetians. Though all were in turn subdued or consolidated in the Roman empire, it was not until the days of Augustus that Rome, which administered the affairs of the world, established at home such a territorial organization as was needed for administrative purposes.

From the Etruscans Rome adopted many of her earlier political institutions; for long before the founding of the eternal city, they were a powerful and civilized nation, skilled in the arts and sciences, especially in vase and mural painting, in the goldsmith's and jeweller's crafts, and in the fashioning of figured mirrors and other useful and ornamental articles in bronze and terra cotta. Among others were Caere, the granary of Etruria, with an abundance of gold and silver deposited in the Delphic treasury, and Pyrgi, the seaport from whose temple Dionysius the tyrant carried away plunder valued at 1,500 talents.

Whence the Etruscans came we know not, for their origin is lost in obscurity; but certain it is that they were a far more civilized race than the Latian, or Latin, tribes among whom the lachrymose hero of the Aeneid cast in his lot, and being slain in battle ascended to heaven, where, let us hope, he was not confronted with his queenly hostess of Carthage, whom he seduced and deserted. After various other traditions comes the founding of Rome, itself in part a tradition, as were the reigns of its earlier and probably of all its kings. Even the date of its founding is uncertain, though as given by Varro, the third year of the sixth Olympiad, or 753 B.C., is also the one adopted by modern historians.

ROMULUS

The age of Romulus, son of Mars and the mythic and eponym founder of Rome — a word meaning strength, and especially brute strength — was one of violence and lawlessness. After despoiling the robber bands of Latium and distributing the booty among his shepherd following, he builds the first wall of the eternal city, for the scorning of which his brother is slain; and not long after his rape of the Sabine women ascends to heaven in a thunder-storm, there to be worshipped as Quirinus, the Sabine name for Mars. Thence he sends word, as Livy relates, that the Romans are destined to become the wealthiest and most powerful nation in the world. Nomos, or law, is personified in his successor Numa, whose election points to a Sabine fusion and perhaps to a Sabine invasion. At this time the nation, if such it can be called, was divided into three tribes and thirty curiae, the former probably a clan division, and the latter consisting of associations bound together by civil duties and religious rites, with common hearth and hall, and with common priests and festivals.

During the reign of Tullus Hostilius, the destruction of Alba and the organization of its citizens as the basis of the plebs, largely increased the power of Rome. At the mouth of the Tiber is established the first Roman Colony, and the port of Ostia is built, together with salt works as a source of revenue to the state.

THE TWIN FOUNDERS OF ROME, CAPITOLINE

4

It is in the reign of Tarquinius Priscus that tradition begins to give way to history, great public works being undertaken in his reign, of which mention will presently be made. Tarquin was an Etruscan by birth, a man of wealth and influence, and as to the story of his life and reign many romantic incidents are related, which need not here detain us. Making war against the remnant of the Sabines and Latins he defeated both these ancient enemies of Rome, completing the conquest of Latium and returning with the spoils of many cities. In the triumph with which he celebrated his victories was more of the glitter of wealth than had ever before been witnessed, the king appearing in a chariot drawn by four white horses and attired in a robe embroidered with flowers of gold. The story of Servius Tullius is also largely in the nature of a romance, except the public improvements and political reforms undertaken during his reign. Tullius was the Solon of the Romans, dividing the people into classes, with rights and privileges determined by property qualifications. In the first class were those whose possessions were valued at 100,000 ases, or $1,600, the amount decreasing until in the fifth or lowest class it was only 12,500 ases or about $200. Then there were the proletarii, whose effects were so slender that they were exempt from tribute, paying only a poll-tax. Thus was wealth computed in Rome during the regal period, when the joint riches of the patrician order would not have furnished forth a single banquet for Nero or Caligula.

With the expulsion of Tarquin the Proud, the monarchy ends, and the republican era is inaugurated amid a general shrinkage of power and territory, Rome, instead of ruling far and wide over Latium and Etruria, sinking into an almost insignificant state, surrounded with hostile and independent tribes. The wealth and splendor which characterized the rule of the Tarquins had been in striking contrast with the simplicity of the earlier kings. By Etruscan architects were erected monuments little inferior to those of the empire; on Rome were lavished by Etruscan lords all the riches and resources of their opulent and civilized nation, and through Etruscan ports her citizens were first brought into direct contact with the Greeks. In addition to the two sovereigns mentioned in Roman annals, it is probable that several Etruscan princes usurped or were elected to the throne, and of these the younger Tarquin was the last, ending his days at Cumae after thrice attempting in vain to recover his kingdom.

The history of the republican era consists almost entirely of the history of its wars, with which we are here but little concerned. The story of the capture of Veii by Camillus in 396 is probably a portion of a poetic legend resembling that of the Trojan war. The plunder, divided among the army, was very large, Camillus sending one-tenth of his share to the temple of Delphi in the shape of a golden bowl several talents in weight, and devoting the remainder to a splendid triumph which aroused the anger of the gods. There is probably more of truth in the sack and destruction of Rome by Brennus, and the ransom of its capitol for 100,000 pounds of gold. Nor can we accept the statement of Livy that, when the treasure was being weighed, Camillus appeared with his avenging host and put the Gauls to rout. Unfortunately for Roman pride, the coins which formed part of the ransom were extremely plentiful in Gaul for many a century afterward. The city was rebuilt within a single year, materials being furnished by the state, and each one allowed to build as he saw fit, on whatever spot he might select. In their dwellings there was neither beauty nor comfort; the streets were narrow and crooked, many of them crossed by open drains, and so not a few of them remained, with the added unsightliness of later artificers, until the great fire in the reign of Nero rendered them incapable of further deformity.

It was not until the middle of the third century, after further wars with the Gauls, the Etruscans, the Samnites, with other Italian tribes, and above all with Pyrrhus, that Rome became undisputed mistress of Italy, her authority acknowledged throughout the peninsula

PYRRHUS

as the head of the Italian confederacy of states. Except Hannibal, Pyrrhus was the most able leader that the Romans encountered, landing in Italy with 25,000 men and routing their legions in two engagements, mainly through the panic created by his elephants. But presently he was himself defeated, retiring on Tarentum, whose request for aid had been the pretext for his invasion, and thence to his home in Epirus. The final submission of Tarentum, one of the wealthiest of Graeco-Italian cities, was followed by a large acquisition of wealth, and thenceforth luxury began to appear among the Romans, but at first in minor degree. Not many years before a Roman senator had lost his seat because, as the censors showed, he possessed silver vessels ten pounds in weight; but now silver plate was plentiful on Roman tables; there were hired actors, dancers, and flute-players, and there were artists and works in art, both Greek and Etruscan, 2,000 statues being carried to Rome from a single Etrurian town. With the influx of Pyrrhic and Tarentine spoils, the capital laid aside its village-like aspect; public buildings were on a grander scale; in the temples were rich stores of treasure, and for the first time in the annals of the republic most of its citizens were comfortably housed and fed.

The first Punic war placed Rome in possession of Sicily after a severe and protracted struggle which completely emptied her treasury. It was during this war that the first regular fleet was built, 100 quinqueremes and 20 triremes being constructed within a few weeks after the timber had been cut from the wooded chain of the Apennines. The wreck of a Carthaginian quinquereme served as a model, and sailors and rowers were trained on scaffolds; for as yet there were no seafaring men among the people. But the Romans were unfortunate with their earlier armadas. After several brilliant victories, the first one was destroyed by storm; the second was defeated; and most of it wrecked, with great loss of treasure gathered from African cities. A third, built by the contributions of private citizens, was more successful, and in 241 its victory virtually ended the war, the Carthaginians paying as indemnity 2,300 talents.

A few years later Sardinia and Corsica were added to the Roman possessions, not without ineffectual protests from Carthage. Presently came the second of the Punic Wars, Hannibal crossing the Alps at the head of his slender force of 26,000 men, with which, but for his delay at Capua, he would probably have realized the dream of his life — to lay waste with fire and sword the city against which he had sworn eternal vengeance. On the Ticino and the Trebia the Roman legions were defeated; at Thrasymene they were massacred, and the way seemed open to the conqueror, who marching on Rome, as was thought, bathed his horses' feet in the choicest vintages of Italy.

Then came the struggles with Philip V of Macedon and Antiochus III of Syria, the former succeeding in purchasing peace for 1,000 talents and the latter for 12,500, with surrender of fleet and territory. In vain did Perseus, son and successor of Philip, strive to rehabilitate the Macedonian empire. The Romans were intent on its destruction, and this they speedily accomplished, later reducing it to a province, while Perseus himself adorned the triumph of Aemilius Paulus, and ended his days in Italy, where his son earned a scanty livelihood as a wood-turner.

A most ignoble use did Aemilius Paulus make of his victory at Pydna. Macedonia he plundered of its treasures, both in the precious metals and in art; the inhabitants he reduced to virtual slavery, forbidding them to fell timber for shipbuilding or to work their mines of gold and silver; yet exacting a heavy tribute from a people thus reduced to poverty and helplessness. Proceeding thence into Greece, he treated with equal severity those who had espoused the cause of Perseus, and even of Pyrrhus a century before. The men of Epirus he ordered to deliver up all their silver and gold, under penalty of death, and this they did promptly enough, thinking to secure their safety. But at a given signal the cohorts fell upon them, and 15,000 Epirots were massacred or sold into slavery, while their towns to the number of seventy were blotted from the face of the earth. The spoils were enormous, and to them were added, not many years later, those which Mummius sent to Rome by shiploads after the sack of Corinth. The treasury was filled to overflowing, as were the pockets of those in charge of affairs, and to the spoliation of Macedonia and Greece was mainly due the enormous wealth of many citizens of the later republic, contrasting sharply with the sordid poverty of the poor; for in ancient Rome there was no middle class.

AEMILIUS PAULUS

The simplicity of early days had now entirely disappeared, and with it the intense patriotism and strict integrity which marked the days of Brutus and his successors. Everything could be had for money, and there was no disgrace in crime or treachery so long as they yielded a profit, the corruption extending alike to senate and people, to the legions and their commanders. Especially was this apparent when Jugurtha, having murdered his rivals, usurped the throne of Numidia, bribing the Roman ambassadors, the Roman generals, and even the commissioners sent to investigate the charges preferred against him. The first Mithridatic war yielded 20,000 talents, most of which was appropriated by Sulla, after being wrung from the people at the point of the sword, completely exhausting the resources of the country. "From the days of Sulla," remarks Sallust, "Roman soldiers began to rob temples, and to confound things sacred and profane." In Greece he gathered enormous spoils, and returning to Rome, where his triumph was one of the most magnificent pageants of the times, issued his famous proscription, followed by the reign of terror, the wholesale massacres and confiscations with which his name has ever been associated. During his dictatorship Sulla held absolute power over the lives and fortunes of every Roman citizen, being virtually emperor rather than dictator. Resigning in 79, he retired to Puteoli, where he ended his days, one of the wealthiest and most infamous, though unquestionably one of the most talented men of his age.

SULLA

It was during the campaigns of Sulla that Pompey first came into notice, rising rapidly in favor, for he was an able and ambitious leader. Elected consul in 70, after his wars in Africa and Spain, the games which he celebrated, lasting an entire fortnight, were the most splendid thus far witnessed in Rome, not even excepting those where Sulla

POMPEY

exhibited one hundred African lions in the arena. After his consulship he rid the Mediterranean of the pirate hordes which for many years had there held control. In addition to more than a thousand vessels, manned with bold and experienced seamen and thoroughly armed and equipped, they had fortresses and warehouses in which to deposit their booty. Not content with robbing merchant vessels, they pillaged the coasts of Italy, plundering towns and farms and sacking the country villas of the wealthy, even within sight of Rome. By the tribunes, vessels, troops, and money without limit were placed at Pompey's command, and within a few weeks the freebooters were driven from the coasts of Spain and the

Pillars of Hercules, from the shores of Italy and Sicily, far into the Cilician sea, where their fleet was exterminated. Submitting to the conqueror, they were treated with leniency; for most of them had been driven to piracy as the only means of earning a livelihood, and many were settled on the public lands, where they became the best of colonists. This was one of the most brilliant of Pompey's exploits, and also one of the few that were entirely unselfish. From the third Mithridatic war and other Asiatic conquests he returned a few years later with additional spoils and tribute, including 6,000 talents from Mithridates himself. Vast sums were added to the public treasure; to every soldier who had fought in his legions were presented 4,500 sesterces, and at his own expense he erected the theatre which bore his name, together with a temple to Minerva.

CRASSUS

Marcus Licinius Crassus, surnamed the Rich, who with Pompey and Caius Julius Caesar formed the coalition known as the first triumvirate, was probably the wealthiest man in Rome, accumulating an enormous fortune by working silver mines and trafficking in slaves and real estate. Elected as Pompey's colleague in the consulship, he had striven to outbid him as a candidate for public favor, distributing corn in unlimited quantities and feasting the people at ten thousand tables. The triumvirs were all-powerful, doing exactly as they pleased, and dividing the empire among them for the better consummation of their

desires. Crassus selected Syria as his province, where as he thought he could gather at will the treasures of Asia. By way of a beginning he plundered the temple of Jerusalem of sacred vessels and ornaments valued at 2,000 talents; but invading Parthia, he was finally sated with gold; for being defeated and captured by Surena, molten gold was poured down his throat.

MARIUS

After the death of Marius, Caesar was chosen as leader of his faction, or rather of its remnants; for most of them had fallen under the proscription of Sulla. He was a man of extravagant personal habits, and still more extravagant in providing for the entertainment of the people; so that when appointed praetor in 61 he found himself $5,000,000 in debt. Spain was his province; but he could not leave Rome without first settling with his creditors, and this he did with the aid of Crassus, though not until a charge of insolvency had been preferred against him. Returning from

Spain with spoils sufficient to pay his debts and to indulge in further extravagances, he was elected to the consulship, enacting measures which pleased the people but offended the senate, especially in his agrarian law, whereby lands in Campania and elsewhere were distributed among 20,000 needy citizens.

Caesar's campaigns in Gaul and Britain added more to the territorial possessions of Rome than to her glory or wealth; for they were undertaken against barbarians, whose lives

were sacrificed by thousands, while on the survivors untold sufferings were inflicted. Yet when finally subdued the Gallic tribes were kindly treated and lived contentedly under the sway of the Romans, whose laws and civilization they were not slow to adopt. After the battle of Pharsalia, where Caesar secured all the treasures of Pompey's camp, he fell a victim to Cleopatra's fascinations, a weakness which almost cost him his life; for an outbreak occurring in Alexandria, he was besieged in his palace, and escaped only by swimming to a ship anchored off the neighboring shore, leaving behind him his purple robe, which the Alexandrians hung as a trophy in their temple. Returning to Rome as dictator, he celebrated a four days' triumph, among those who followed his car being Arsinoe, sister of

JULIUS CAESAR   Cleopatra, and Vercingetorix, prince of the Arverni, who for a time had caused his star to pale. Then came public feasting at the dictator's expense, with liberal distributions of corn and money, followed by magnificent games such as never before had been held in Rome, After governing for less than two years the world which he had conquered, Caesar meets his fate at the hands of the republican nobles, leaving the bulk of his vast treasures and estates to his adopted son and heir Octavius, the emperor Augustus that was to be, and the world opens under new developments.

In the contentions which followed the death of Julius, Mark Antony was for a time the central figure. As consul in 44 he had been Caesar's colleague, and he it was who by his offer of the crown only a month before had unconsciously hastened the tragedy of the Ides of March. After the battle of Pharsalia he ruled almost as a despot, making a new partition of the provinces and pretending that he did everything in accordance with Caesar's will. But presently Octavius returns to the capital, and though but nineteen years of age is hailed by the legions as successor to his granduncle, assuming the name of Caius Julius Caesar Octavianus. First he demands the treasure bequeathed him by will, together with that which was left as the people's inheritance, all of which had been intrusted to Antony's keeping. But Antony has already squandered most of it in dissipation or

MARK ANTONY,
VATICAN

in the payment of his enormous debts, and is unwilling to part with the remainder. Though finally compelled to do so, it is not until after a serious breach with Octavian, healed for a time by the alliance known as the second triumvirate, in which Lepidus was the third party, though little better than a figure-head.

The breach between Octavian and Antony was renewed by the Cleopatra episode, and widened into open rupture when the latter put away his wife Octavia in favor of the Egyptian concubine on whom he had lavished his treasures and provinces. In Rome he was held in contempt; for after his legions had narrowly escaped destruction at the hands of the

Parthians, he celebrated a magnificent triumph at Alexandria for some petty victory over the Armenians, and then became merely the slave of his mistress, giving himself up to oriental luxury and excess. War was declared against him, and at Actium came the trial of strength, with the result that all the world knows, Octavian, after settling the affairs of the east, returning to Rome with enormous stores of treasure, to be distributed among the legions and the body of the people, together with large donations of land. While celebrating a threefold triumph, he soothed the pride of the nobles by maintaining the outward forms of consular government, himself for the fifth time holding office as consul, to which he was first elected at the age of twenty. Though long before saluted by the legions as imperator, he is presently invested with that title by the senate, and the days of republican Rome are ended.

When securely established on the throne, with the authority of tribune for life, to which, after the death of Lepidus, was added that of pontifex maximus, Octavian presently assumed his title of Augustus, a word applied to Roman temples and rites and to all that was held most sacred and venerable. His reign was devoted to improving the condition of the people, in the provinces as well as in the capital, constructing roads and bridges, reclaiming lands, and erecting public buildings, all attended with a liberal but judicious

APPIAN WAY

expenditure. It was for the metropolis that Augustus reserved his munificence, rearing the most imposing and costly monuments of the empire, and in such number that, as he declared, "he found Rome a city of brick and left it one of marble." By Julius many of these works had been planned, and had he lived, would doubtless have been executed during his reign; for never before had public funds been so abundant. After presenting 20,000 sesterces to every soldier who had fought on his side in the civil war, with a liberal donation to Roman citizens and other large payments that need not here he specified, there remained in the national treasury 700,000,000 sesterces, and in his own 100,000,000, equivalent in all to $40,000,000, or ten times as much as had ever before been at the disposal of the republic. In addition to the spoils of conquered nations, the revenues had been largely increased by the taxes imposed on them, and by the forced loans, fines, and penalties exacted from wealthy individuals, certain African capitalists, for instance, being mulcted in 100,000,000 sesterces merely for siding with the opposition senate. All this, with later additions, was now at the disposal of Augustus, to be applied to the great works and monuments of his time, in the description of which will here be included those of earlier and later eras.

During the regal and consular periods, there were few imposing structures in Rome, chief among them being the wall of Servius, the temple of Jupiter Capitolinus, the forum, the theatre of Pompey, the curia, and on the Appian way the dome of Caecilia Metella. To these may be added the aqueducts and the Cloaca Maxima, while the spacious and substantial roads converging on the capital from every portion of the empire, and of which not a few remain, were more remarkable than all the rest. "Three things," said Dionysius of Halicarnassus, "reveal the magnificence of Rome, her aqueducts, her roads, and her drains."

The principal roads, or viae stratae as they were termed, were constructed of blocks of basalt, carefully fitted together on beds resembling those which are used for mosaic pavements. Most famous of all was the Appia via, which Horace calls the regina viarum, or queen of roads, begun by the censor Appius Claudius, and later extended to Brundusium, with a total length of 350 miles. By Appius was also built the first of the great aqueducts

which conducted to Rome the water of neighboring hills, the remainder, thirteen in number, being for the most part erected on triumphal arches, the ruins of which are among the most imposing in the Campagna. The largest of the aqueducts, begun by Caligula and completed by Claudius, after whom it was named, was 40 miles in length, and at such a level as to convey water to all the hills on which Rome was built. Its cost was 350,000,000 sesterces or

CLAUDIAN AQUEDUCT

$17,500,000, most of this amount being expended on the arches as the Romans knew but little of hydrostatics. The earliest of Roman bridges was the Pons Sublicius, so called from the subliciae or piles on which it was built. It was a wooden drawbridge merely; for Rome was as yet by no means safe from attack, the Tiber being regarded as its strongest defence, and it was not until after the final overthrow of Hannibal put an end to all fear of invasion that the first stone bridge was erected — the Pons Lapidaeus or Pons Aemilius, the latter from the name of its founder. The Ponte Rotto now occupies its site, and still in use is the Pons Fabricius, a massive structure of tufa and peperino, faced with travertine, which about 60 B.C. first connected the city with the Insula Tiberina. Well preserved also are the Pons Cestius, spanning the river between the island and the Janiculan shore, and the Pons Aelius, now the Ponte Saint Angelo, which led from Hadrian's mausoleum to the Campus Martius.

By Servius Tullius were established the dimensions of Rome as they existed under the republic, the Viminal and Esquiline mounts being added to the five fortified hills which formed the inhabited portion, that is to say the Capitoline, Quirinal, Palatine, Aventine, and Coelian, thus completing what was termed the Sepimontium. Of all the remains of the regal period the most striking are those of what is commonly known as the wall of Servius, though portions of it belong to earlier and later dates. Starting from the Tiber, it extended in a straight line to the Capitoline and thence to the Quirinal and other hills, though not forming a complete circuit, for each of them had its own fortifications, which so far as possible were utilized for the work. It was built of tufa blocks, probably quarried on the spot, two Roman feet in thickness, and laid in alternate courses. The arched openings, the uses of which cannot be determined, were of harder material, with blocks of great length, bevelled and set in mortar. In front were an agger and a foss 100 feet wide and 30 in depth, the wall being strengthened with massive buttresses to resist the pressure of the earth. In the days of Augustus the agger was converted into a public walk, and the foss tilled in and afterward built upon, while the main structure was used for the back walls of houses, some of which, still in existence, display thereupon the painted stucco work of the time of Hadrian.

Still in existence are considerable portions of the great walls of Aurelian, some twelve miles in circumference and enclosing the fourteen thickly populated regions or districts into which the city and its suburbs were divided by Augustus. The work was undertaken as a protection against the assaults of German and Gothic hordes, when the legions were required for distant portions of the empire. By Probus the walls were completed and by Arcadius and Honorius strengthened by gate-towers, Theodoric, Belisarius, and later the supreme pontiffs restoring and preserving them throughout the middle ages. The circuit was broken by various buildings, and by the projection where was the Praetorian camp, of whose fortifications there are many remains, including one of its principal gates.

The tomb of Caecilia Metella, "the stern round tower of other days," as Byron terms it, was nearly 100 feet in diameter, and yet of such massive construction that the internal chamber was barely twenty feet in width. Of Roman tombs, and especially those of circular form, there are many striking remains, especially those of Hadrian's mausoleum, now converted into the castle of St. Angelo, where were the marble columns and domed roof of an edifice 170 feet square at the base. Cremation was common with the Romans, and among wealthy families the ashes of the deceased or the sarcophagus which contained his corpse, of which latter that of the Scipios is a familiar example, were enclosed in buildings of imposing structure and elegant design.

FORUM ROMANUM SHOWING EXCAVATIONS

The Forum Romanum, or Forum Magnum as it was afterward called to distinguish it from the fora of the empire, lay in the valley, or rather the swamp between the Capitoline and Palatine mounts. It was roughly built and of quadrangular shape, its longer sides being flanked by butchers' and tradesmen's stalls, while on the northern face were the quarters of the silver-smiths. Here, after the marshy ground had been drained by cloacae, was the favorite site for commercial transactions, for political gatherings, and for scenic and gladiatorial exhibitions, for which a central space was reserved, though later inconveniently crowded with statues and monuments. The forum was for centuries the meeting-place of the comitia tributa, or plebs, and on the comitium adjoining, a level space on which the curia fronted, was the rendezvous of the patricians or comitia curiata. In the curia, or senate-house, founded, as was the forum, and probably completed by Servius Tullius, were usually held the sessions of the senate until its destruction by fire in 52 B.C. During this and later periods, however, these sessions were frequently held in one of the temples, but never in the aedes sacrae, or sacred edifices devoted exclusively to religious purposes. The curia was several times rebuilt; first by the son of Sulla, who named it after his gens the curia Cornelia; then by Augustus who styled it the Curia Julia; a third time by Domitian and finally by Diocletian. By one of the supreme pontiffs it was converted into the church of Saint Adriano, and by Alexander VII its bronze doors were used for the nave of the Lateran basilica.

First among the five imperial fora was that which Julius Caesar founded to commemorate the battle of Pharsalia. Together with its central fane of Venus Genitrix, it was completed by Augustus, and was one of the most costly of Roman structures; for it was built in a crowded quarter, and as Cicero relates, 100,0000,000 sesterces, or $5,000,000 was paid for the site alone. Adjoining it was the forum of Augustus, in which was a temple of Mars the avenger,

BAS RELIEF, FORUM ROMANUM

erected in token of the vengeance inflicted on the assassins of his great-uncle. It was enclosed by a wall 100 feet in height, the remains of which are among the most imposing ruins of ancient Rome, and still in existence are three of the marble Corinthian columns with their entablatures which formed a portion of the peristyle. Of the walls and arch of Vespasian's Forum Pacis, burned to the ground during the reign of Commodus and restored by Severus, there are also massive remains, and especially of the addition made by Maxentius in the shape of a circular structure fronting on the Sacra Via. The original building was probably used as a hall of records; and here also was one of the finest of Roman temples, in which was a large and valuable art collection, including statues by Phidias and Lysippus.

The forum of Nerva, usually called the Forum Palladium from its temple of Pallas, was lined with marble and adorned with rows of Corinthian pillars, on a remnant of whose entablature are represented in relief the industrial arts of which Minerva was the patron goddess. In the reign of Alexander Severus were grouped around it colossal statues of the emperors who had been deified, together with columns inscribed with their exploits. Largest among the imperial fora, and one of the finest in architectural design, was

FORUM OF TRAJAN

that on which were expended during the reign of Trajan seventeen years of time and an enormous sum of money. To make room for its site was cut away a large spur of hill that connected the Quirinal with the Capitoline mount. Its principal entrance was in the form of a triumphal arch, whose figures in relief were afterward used for the arch of Constantine, the sides of its peristyle and curved projections being lined with shops. Opposite are the column of Trajan, on which are represented his Dacian victories, and the remains of the Basilica Ulpia, with its handsome pavement of oriental marble, where were two of the largest libraries in Rome. Finally there were, in addition to those already mentioned, the Forum Piscarium, Pistorium, and Olitorium; that is to say the fish, bread, and oil markets.

In Rome were many temples, and especially on the Capitoline hill, whose peaks, called the Capitolium and the Arx, with the valley that lay between, and in truth the entire mount, were crowded in the time of the empire with magnificent architectural and artistic monuments enriched with the spoils of the Hellenic world. Here was the triumphal arch in honor of Nero, with much statuary and other works of art. Here was the temple of Fides which Numa founded, and which, when rebuilt during the first of the Punic wars, was spacious enough for meetings of the senate, as also was the fane of Honos et Virtus, erected by Marius, that of Jupiter Tonans, reared by Augustus, being of smaller and more graceful dimensions.

By the first of the Tarquins was founded and by his son was built in the Etruscan style of architecture the vast triple edifice commonly known as the temple of Jupiter Capitolinus, though dedicated also, as were other Etruscan fanes, to Juno and Minerva. It was in the basement or rather in a subterraneous cell of this temple that the Sibylline books were preserved, of which we have the familiar story of the sibyl and the king, the latter paying 300 pieces of gold for the three remaining books, after the sibyl, at first turned away in scorn, had burned six out of the nine offered for the same amount. Though on its construction were expended the rich spoils of the Volscian war and the taxes and enforced labor of Roman citizens, it was but a plain and almost unsightly building, with facades of painted and stuccoed peperino, wooden architraves, and statues of terra cotta. Burned to the ground some four centuries later, it was replaced by an imposing structure of marble, with Corinthian columns from the Athenian temple of Olympian Jove, erected by Sulla, Catulus, and Augustus, the name of Catulus only, by whom it was completed and dedicated, appearing above its portal. Not many years later it was demolished by rioters, and after being rebuilt by Vespasian was again destroyed during the reign of Titus, in the great conflagration of 79. This also is the date of the eruption which buried Herculaneum and Pompeii beneath the ashes and lava of Vesuvius, and it was while the emperor was viewing the scene of desolation and contributing generously to the relief of the distressed that the catastrophe occurred in Rome. Finally, in the time of Domitian, the temple was once more rebuilt, and for centuries was acknowledged as one of the most striking of Roman monuments. Its peristyle, in the form of a double colonnade, was of Pentelic marble, and on the gilding alone was expended, as Plutarch relates, $12,500,000, the gilt bronze tiles forming a portion of the spoils which fell to Genseric the Visigoth.

TEMPLE OF VESTA

Another great temple was the one which Camillus erected on the Arx in honor of Juno Moneta, or Juno the Adviser. It was afterward converted into a mint, and hence it was, as Livy opines, that the word moneta was used to signify money. On its site now stands the church of Ara Coeli, and on that of the fane of Jupiter Capitolinus, the Palazzo Cafarelli.

Elsewhere in Rome were numerous temples erected at various dates, though such as belong to the earlier period, as those of Janus and Vesta, had little to commend them either in structure or design. The former was in truth little more than a gateway near the forum, and the latter was but a plain circular edifice, though the most hallowed of Roman shrines,

TEMPLE OF SATURN

containing as it did the sacred fire and relics on which, as was supposed, the fate of the kingdom depended. It was several times destroyed, and finally rebuilt by Severus, with dome of Syracusan bronze symbolizing the canopy of heaven. Adjoining it was the Atrium Vestae, where dwelt the vestal virgins in small apartments fronting on the quadrangle, while the larger chambers were floored with mosaic work and lined with the rarest and most beautiful of polished marbles. The original structure was, however, of a more primitive character; for the home of the vestals, like the temple, was more than once demolished and restored. The last restoration was in the time of Hadrian, excavations made in 1883 disclosing many interesting remains, among them a vessel containing nearly a thousand English pennies of ninth and tenth century coinage — the Peter's pence to Rome.

In the purest of Grecian style was the temple of Castor, rebuilt during the reign of Augustus on the site of the sorry looking structure erected live centuries before to commemorate the victory at Lake Regillus. Exceedingly graceful and delicate are the three Corinthian columns of Pentelic marble which form the most valuable among the remains. In the building itself is a striking example of the solidity of Roman architecture, massive walls of tufa, eight feet in thickness, supporting the cellae and columns, while the podium is filled with concrete solid as a rock, its surface forming an elevated platform on which the superstructure is reared. In the basement, as in other temples, — those of Saturn and Concord, for instance — were vaults in which money, jewelry, and plate were stored for safe-keeping, a custom which the Romans appear to have adopted from the Greeks.

The temple of Concord, rebuilt by Tiberius and Drusus on the site of the structure which Camillus founded, was lined throughout with white and oriental marbles, its door-sill fashioned of huge marble blocks on which rested a bronze caduceus, emblem of peace. Within was

TEMPLE OF VENUS

a magnificent collection of paintings, statuary, engraved gems, and costly plate, for the most part the workmanship of Greek artists and workers in art. The tympanum was covered with sculptures; the portico was filled with statues, and of the rich Corinthian entablature many fragments are still preserved. Close at hand was the temple of Vespasian, also lined with marble, and with an internal range of Corinthian columns, as in the fane of Concord.

The largest of Roman temples was that of Venus Felix, on an outlying spur of the Palatine known as the Velia, near which are exposed for a height of 20 or 30 feet the foundations of the Golden House of Nero. Around it were Corinthian columns of Pentelic marble, and an outer colonnade with nearly 200 pillars of granite and porphyry, of which a

PANTHEON

few fragments still remain, together with portions of the cellae, where were colossal figures of the goddess. Designed by Hadrian and probably completed by Antoninus Pius, it was partially destroyed and in part restored in the reign of Maxentius, its restoration being continued by Constantine. For centuries its remains were utilized as a quarry, the marble being converted into lime in kilns constructed of broken pieces of porphyry, while the gilt bronze tiles which covered the roof were used by Pope Honorius I for the basilica of St. Peter's.

Of all the great monuments of the empire the Pantheon of Agrippa in the Campus Martius is the best preserved, still remaining almost in its entirety. Though portions of it belonged to the system of thermae planned by Agrippa, the huge round structure which formed the Pantheon proper, its enormous dome, 142 feet in span resting on a podium 73 feet in height, and seemingly balanced in air, was consecrated to the gods from whom was traced the ancestry of the Caesars. The dome was lighted at the apex by an aperture so far above ground that in the most violent storm not a breath of wind was felt by those who

INTERIOR OF PANTHEON

stood beneath, the rain falling vertically upon the pavement, where it traced a circle 30 feet in diameter. For the covering of the dome and the ceiling of the portico, in rear of which stood colossal statues of Augustus and Agrippa, were used 450,000 pounds of Syracusan bronze, the ceiling being supported by massive girders, afterward melted and cast into cannon for the fortress of Saint Angelo. The walls were of tufa concrete, lined with brick and nearly 20 feet in thickness; the larger columns were of granite, with others of white marble, and on the tympanum were figures in relief representing the conflict between the gods and giants. In the interior were oriental marbles and colored porphyries in great variety, some of them belonging to the restorations of Hadrian and Severus, and within recent years have been disclosed the remains of a grand hall with Corinthian pillars supporting a richly sculptured entablature, forming a part of the thermae which later became the pride of Rome.

The first of some forty triumphal arches were erected nearly two hundred years before the Christian era in the Circus Maximus and the Forum Boarium from the spoils

ARCH OF TITUS

which Stertinius gathered in Spain. In Domitian's arch of Titus and Vespasian on the Sacra Via, probably the earliest specimen of the composite order, is represented the triumphal procession held after the conquest of Judaea, with Titus and his chariot carved in relief on the inner side, and on the exterior, soldiers bearing the trumpets, the golden candlestick, and other sacred articles taken from the temple at Jerusalem. Of the arch of Marcus Aurelius, which spanned what is now the Corso, some of its finest reliefs have been preserved in the Capitoline museum. Of existing arches, the one which Constantine erected near the Colosseum is perhaps the finest, though owing none of its beauties to this period of art degradation; for not only

the entire design but the reliefs and other decorative features are taken from the structure which Trajan reared as an entrance way to his forum.

The marble pedestal of Antonine's column, a granite monolith surmounted by a colossal gilt-bronze statue, is among the Vatican collection, as also is a fragment of the shaft, with an inscription stating that it was fashioned in the ninth year of Trajan's reign, the remainder of the material being used to repair the obelisk which Augustus erected in

the Campus Martius. The Trajan and Aurelian columns were both more than 100 feet in height, the latter, which stood in front of the temple of Aurelius, also with its colossal statue and with spiral reliefs in twenty tiers representing the emperor's victories in Germany.

The palace of Augustus, with the adjacent temple and libraries of Apollo, contained in the Area Apollinis, occupied the centre of the Palatine hill, of which, as of Rome itself, this costly and magnificent group, stored with the choicest productions of Greek artists and art workers in gold and silver, in ivory, bronze, and marble, was the chief architectural ornament. Of the palace itself, which stood on the edge of the cliff, facing the Circus Maximus, but little is known except what Ovid tells us; for none of it is now above

ARCH OF AUGUSTUS

ground, though drawings still in existence show the results of excavations made in 1775. The temple, on the building of which were expended eight years of time and money without stint, was approached through propylaea no less imposing than those of the Athenian Acropolis and through a Portico with more than fifty fluted columns of Numidian and Grecian marble, between which were statues of the Danaids and their bridegrooms. In front was a shrine of Vesta and an altar surrounded with oxen in bronze, the latter the workmanship of Myron, one of the foremost sculptors of the school to which Phidias belonged. On the door was represented in ivory reliefs the death of the Niobids; around the walls were statues of the muses, and in the cella those of Apollo by Scopas and of Latona by Praxiteles, with others in gold and silver and a choice collection of precious stones presented by Marcellus. Of Augustus an inscription records that he sold eighty silver images of himself, presented by his admirers, and with the proceeds dedicated golden gifts to this fane which he reared to the glory of Apollo and of Augustus. Flanking the portico were the libraries, one containing works in Latin and the other in Greek, forming together what was then the best collection extant of classic literature. Finally there was a spacious hall where at times the senate held its sessions, and in the centre of which stood a colossal statue of the emperor fifty feet in height.

The palace Of Caligula, while one of the largest and most costly, was also one of the most unsightly structures on the Palatine hill, where the mansions of many wealthy

PALACE OF CALIGULA

Romans, purchased at enormous cost, were all insufficient for this unwieldy edifice. Extended on lofty arches over the Clivus Victoriae, its substructures were of gigantic proportions, built probably for the purpose of raising the upper rooms to a level with the summit of the mount. Portions of the ground floor would appear to have been used as shops; for still may be traced the wide openings that contained the wooden fronts, then characteristic of Roman as now of eastern stores and warehouses. Above them were chambers lined with marble and rich in columnar and mosaic decorations, of which only the merest fragments remain.

The Flavian palace, with its imposing peristyle, its outer colonnades, its walls and floors all of the finest oriental marble, polished in brilliant hues, was filled with Greek statuary, of which many specimens, unearthed during the excavations ordered by the duke of Parma early in the eighteenth century, are still preserved in the museums of Naples. The choicest among them were in the throne-room and the basilica, the plan of the latter being afterward adopted in the Christian basilica, presently to be described. The entire building was used only for state occasions, the emperor himself residing in the palace of Caligula, with which it was connected by a subterranean passage.

By Hadrian was almost completed the Stadium Palatinum founded by Domitian and later altered by Severus. Adjoining it was the palace of Hadrian, with richly decorated chambers, one of which, overlooking the race course, is still in a fair state of preservation. As compared with other of the imperial mansions, it was neither a large nor costly building, though one of the most artistic and sightly structures on the Palatine hill. Hadrian was himself an artist and a lover of art for its own sake, as well as for the lustre which it conferred on the empire, superintending in person the public monuments with which he adorned the capital and other portions of his domain, From the extensive remains of his villa near Tivoli, itself a work of art, have been transferred to the Vatican many beautiful specimens of ornamental sculpture and of statues and groups in marble, bronze, and granite, forming portions of a magnificent collection made during his progress through the provinces.

In height, as in superficial area, the palace of Severus was of enormous proportions, covering the southeastern angle of the Palatine and thence extending far into the valley of the Circus Maximus, the latter portion raised on substructures from the base to more than a hundred feet above the level of the mount. Adjoining it were spacious bath-rooms lined with marble and richly decorated with mosaics, water being supplied from the conduit which Nero built as an extension of the Claudian aqueduct. At the foot of the hill stood the Septizonium, a seven-story building with elaborate ornamentation, which Severus dedicated to the sun and moon. During the pontificate of Sixtus V that which remained of it was

ARCH OF SEVERUS

destroyed, its marble columns and other embellishments being used for the new basilica of St. Peter.

Until near the close of the consular period there were few costly and pretentious mansions in Rome; for as yet there was no great accumulation of riches. In the consulship of Lepidus, one of the wealthiest of Roman citizens, there was not in the capital, as Pliny relates, a finer residence than that of Lepidus himself; and yet within thirty years from that period there were at least a hundred that surpassed it in magnificence. "Let a person take into consideration," says Pliny, "the vast masses of marble, the productions of painters, the regal treasures that must have been expended in bringing these hundred mansions to vie with one that had been in its day the most sumptuous and the most celebrated in all the city; then let him reflect that since that time these have again been far excelled by others without number."

Though with many exceptions, the mansions of the wealthy and noble were for the most part of plain exterior, decorative effect being reserved for the internal portions. The chambers were of no great size and usually windowless, although the Romans understood the manufacture of glass, the best of them containing paintings, arabesques, and architectural ornamentations. The houses of the plebeians were of brick, fronting on narrow, irregular, and ill-paved streets, and often negligently built by speculative and dishonest contractors, with the result that the former were reduced to beggary and the latter became exceedingly rich. While towering above them were here and there a few pretentious structures, with porticos and perhaps with facades of marble, the boast of Augustus that he found Rome a city of brick and left it one of marble was true in the main only of its public buildings.

As a rule the man of wealth regarded his city residence merely as a place in which to eat and sleep and decently entertain his friends, expending his means on a costly villa

SALLUST

either in the neighborhood of Rome or near some favorite resort. Cicero for instance had his Formian villa, and Sallust a country home which he loved even better than his famous gardens on the Quirinal, while Lucullus, whom Pompey named the Roman Xerxes, had his parks and mansions at Tusculum, where on a single banquet he would expend 200,000 sesterces. "In the domains of Tusculum and Tibur," says Mommsen, speaking of

CICERO,
UFFIZI GALLERY

a somewhat later era, "on the shores of Tarracina and Baiae, where the old Latin and Italian farmers had sown and reaped, there now rose in barren splendor the villas of the Roman nobles, some of which covered the space of a moderate sized town with their appurtenances of garden grounds and aqueducts, fresh and salt-water ponds for the preservation and breeding of river and marine fishes, nurseries of snails and slugs, game-preserves for keeping hares, rabbits, stags, roes, and wild boars, and aviaries in which even cranes and peacocks were kept. But the luxury of a great city enriches also many an industrious hand, and supports more poor than philanthropy with its expenditure of alms. The aviaries and fish-ponds of the grandees were of course under ordinary circumstances a very costly indulgence; but this system was carried to such an extent that the stock of a pigeon-house was valued at 100,000 sesterces." However beneficial this extravagance may have been to those whom the wealthy patronized or employed, it was not so with the masses of the people; for in the closing decades of the republic agriculture was simply crowded out of the land, while for want of skilled workmen there were few manufactures or other important industries. Thus it was that in Rome there were virtually only two classes — the rich who revelled in luxury and the poor who lived in abject poverty, depending on donations from the public treasury or from those whom their votes had helped to rob the treasury.

In this community of mendicants and millionaires there were more than 300,000 persons entitled to the distributions of food for which no payment was expected. For those who worked with their hands the daily wage did not average more than three sesterces or fifteen cents a day, thus driving many into the army for the sake of its pay and perquisites; for as in the days of Napoleon military service was the royal road to wealth. As for the rest, they formed the idle and criminal element, the rabble or proletariat of Rome.

While the possessions of wealthy Romans contrast somewhat feebly with those of modern millionaires, they were nevertheless considerable and somewhat widely distributed, at least two thousand citizens being accounted as wealthy. In the days of Marius an estate of 2,000,000 sesterces, or $100,000, was accounted as riches; but a few years later the standard was largely increased. Crassus, the richest of all the Romans, except perhaps Lucullus, began life with $350,000, and after distributing enormous sums in entertaining the people, died worth $8,500,000. The property left by Pompey was purchased for $3,500,000; Ahenobarbus, to whose family Nero belonged, distributed allotments of land among 20,000 soldiers without impairing his estate; Aesop the actor, a contemporary of Roscius, was worth $1,000,000, and there were many who by farming, traffic, and money-lending accumulated what were then considered as enormous sums. Others who afterward secured princely fortunes commenced their career with princely liabilities; Julius Caesar owing, as I have said, $1,000,000 to $1,250,000; Mark Antony $2,000,000, and the partisan leader Milo $3,500,000. Politics were then, as today, an expensive pastime, for all the higher offices were sold to the highest bidder, as much as $500,000 being paid for the consulship, which lasted but for a single year.

The highest price paid for a Roman mansion, so far as recorded, was $750,000; but there were probably few that cost more than half that amount. For country villas and their appurtenances $200,000 may be stated as an average outlay, and of these at least two were maintained by the wealthier grandees; one in the mountains near Rome and another at Baiae, Puteoli, or elsewhere on the Campanian coast. Their furniture was of the most costly description, $50,000 being paid for a single table fashioned of African cyprus. At their banquets guests reclined on lounges mounted in silver, and of silver were the shelves

AN IMPERIAL PALACE

of the banqueting hall and even the kitchen utensils. The fashionable Roman dressed in purple attire, the folds of which were carefully adjusted before the mirror. Jewels and pearls had taken the place of simple golden ornaments, and these were in such profusion that at the triumph of Pompey his image was displayed entirely wrought in pearls.

In nothing did extravagance run to such excess as in the luxury of the table, the entire villa being arranged with a view to the feasts which were almost of daily occurrence. Land and sea were ransacked to provide new dainties and delicacies for the jaded appetites of Roman epicures and gourmands. From Chalcedon came tunny-fish; from Tarentum oysters, and from the straits of Gades purple shell-fish; there were grouse from Phrygia; peacocks from Samos, and cranes from the island of Melos, with chickens, ducks, and hares dressed in the highest style of culinary art, while Egypt and Spain furnished the choicest of fruits and nuts. Foreign wines only were drunk, especially those of Sicily, Chios, and Lesbos, of which enormous stocks were kept in the cellars of the rich, the orator Hortensius, for instance, whose forty years of practice had brought him enormous wealth, leaving to his heir 10,000 jars or more than 80,000 gallons of the choicest of Grecian and other vintages.

First of all the lessons learned by those who aspired to office in Rome was that the people must be amused and fed, both free of cost or nearly so. Thus in the earlier days of the empire, when the wealth of the world was concentrated in the imperial city, enormous sums were expended on the support and entertainment of the populace, distributions of money being frequent, while daily or weekly distributions of grain were regarded as a matter of course, and to these oil and wine were not infrequently added. Living as they did almost at the public expense, or rather at the expense of the emperors, the poorer citizens had much idle time on their hands, and this they were never at a loss how to spend. For a small copper coin they could enjoy all the luxury of the thermae or public baths, with their libraries, art galleries, and gymnasia. Without payment of any kind they might sit all day, as often they did, in the Circus Maximus, which to them was their home and temple, the very centre and heart of Rome, as Rome was the centre of the world. Long before dawn an impatient crowd was assembled, intent on securing places, and many there were who passed a sleepless night in the porticos adjacent. From morn till eve, heedless of summer heats or winter rains, spectators to the number of a quarter of a million or more remained in rapt attention, their gaze intent on horses and charioteers while alternating between hope and fear for the success of their favorite champions, as though the fate of the empire depended on the issue of a race.

The Circus Maximus was the most ancient structure of its kind in Rome; for the original building was erected, as is supposed, by the younger Tarquin, though it was not until the fourth century that horse and chariot racing was introduced. After being many times altered and enlarged, and more than once partially destroyed by fire, it was finally completed by Constantine, with facade of marble and sloping tiers of marble seats, of which the lower row were reserved for persons of rank. Long before his reign the combats of gladiators and of men with beasts had given place to chariot and other racing. The chariots passed seven times round the course, and to avoid the goal at either end — the meta fervidis evitata rotis, as Horace puts it — was the test of the driver's skill. They were usually drawn by two or four horses, and sometimes was combined with these exhibitions a race of riders who leaped from the hack of one steed to another. Most of the drivers were slaves, and with the horses, equipage, and attendants, were furnished by wealthy owners of studs, who doubtless found their pastime as expensive as the horse-breeding and horse-racing of the present day. Among other Roman circi was that of Caligula and Nero in the gardens of Agrippina at the foot of the Vatican hill, where now stands the sacristy of St. Peter's.

By the aedile Marcus Scaurus was erected, merely for temporary use, a theatre which Pliny terms the greatest work ever accomplished by the hands of man. It was of three stories, and supported on 360 columns, and between them brazen statues, 3,000 in number. The lowest story was walled with marble, the second with glass, and the third with gilded wood, seats being provided for 80,000 spectators.

Pompey's theatre, in which was the fanes of Venus Victrix and Roma Aeterna, and in front a portico of a hundred columns, was the first one built of stone; for in republican Rome there was a prejudice against the permanent temples of the drama which found favor with the Greeks. In close proximity was the curia of Pompey, where Cesar was assassinated. In the middle of the sixteenth century the colossal statue at the base of which he expired, now standing in the Palazzo Spada, was unearthed in the neighborhood of its site, as also, some fifty years ago, was the huge bronze statue of Hercules, — a third century work — whose present home is in the Vatican. After Caesar's death the theatre was burned to the ground by order of the senate, and the spot where it stood declared forever accursed. It was restored, however, by Augustus, and after being twice again consumed was rebuilt by Titus, with accommodation, as Pliny relates, for 40,000 spectators. Some portions only of its foundations remain; but of the theatre of Marcellus, completed

TITUS

by his uncle Augustus, a well preserved remnant of the external arcade shows that it was mainly of the Ionic order, and with architectural details of remarkable delicacy. As Pliny would have us believe, two contiguous theatres built of wood, placed back to back, and when filled with spectators revolving on pivots so as to enclose an arena where gladiators fought were constructed by Scribonius Curio with the aid of Julius Caesar. More probable is the story that Caesar placed at the disposal of his friend Aemilius Paulus 8,000,000 sesterces wherewith to build the Basilica Julia, completed by Augustus and containing innumerable pillars of the finest Phrygian marble. By Julius was erected the first regular amphitheatre, followed by those of Caligula and Nero, all of wood and used for wild beast and gladiatorial exhibitions. The first one of stone was the Colosseum, so called from the colossus or colossal statue in the porch of Nero's Golden House, 120 feet in height, so altered by Vespasian as to resemble Apollo, and removed by Hadrian to the neighborhood of the great edifice whose ruins are still regarded with a feeling akin to awe. Built by Vespasian and Titus, and restored by Alexander Severus after being partially destroyed by fire, the Colosseum was elliptical in shape, with the longer axial line 620 feet and the shorter 515 feet in length, and an arena about 250 by 170 feet, though the dimensions of the latter are variously stated. It was 180 feet in height; profusely decorated with Doric, Ionic, and Corinthian columns, and covered with an awning to protect from sun and rain the 110,000 spectators for whom seating and standing room was provided. The lowest of the ranges of seats, all of them concentric with the four stages of the external elevation, was called the podium, where sat the emperor, the senators, and the chief magistrates. Above were three galleries, of which the lowest was appropriated to the equestrian order, all being provided with passages, stairways, and covered corridors.

COLOSSEUM

The arena, so called from the sand with which it was strewn, though some of the emperors used costly powders and even gold dust as a substitute, was enclosed with a wall of polished marble and a metal railing for protection against savage beasts. From hidden tubes a spray of scented liquids was scattered at times over the spectators, to neutralize, probably, the effect of imperfect ventilation and of the close, hot atmosphere breathed by the packed and sweltering multitude, protected only by an awning from the rays of a midsummer sun. In addition to the well-known entertainments, of which the massacre of Christians were most in favor, other attractions were produced, some of them difficult to explain, as the mimic fights between vessels of war that occasionally

MARS

followed the regular exhibitions. Until the eighth century at least the Colosseum was still intact; but in common with other ancient buildings was later used as a quarry, Michael Angelo being one of its despoilers and freely using its materials for the building of a Roman palace. Elsewhere in Italy were other amphitheatres, many of them resembling the Colosseum in general features, though not of course in size. Among them was that of Fidenae, by the collapse of which, during the reign of Tiberius, 50,000 persons were killed or injured, and the one at Pompeii, pictured in the pages of Bulwer Lytton's romance.

During the empire the accumulations of statues and paintings were on an enormous scale, those of the regal and republican periods being now regarded merely as of sacred or archaeological interest. Not only had the

FLORA

principal cities of Greece, of Magna Graecia, Sicily, and Asia Minor been despoiled of their choicest treasures, but from the hands of Greek artists residing in the capital were innumerable copies of the more valuable works, many of them now preserved in the Vatican and other museums. They were of all materials, hundreds being of gold and ivory and thousands of silver, while those of marble and bronze outnumbered all the rest. In the mansions of the wealthy there were many libraries, and for wealthy authors, of whom there were not a few, household slaves made copies of their works for distribution among their friends.

CALIGULA

To return to the emperors; by Caligula were squandered the vast stores of wealth left by his predecessor Tiberius, who managed the finances of the empire with economy. While distributing large donations among the people, and amusing them with costly games, Caligula squandered enormous sums on himself, his vices and his whims, sometimes in such wanton fashion that men said his mind was affected. He ordered, for instance, a bridge to be built from Baiae to Puteoli, merely that he might boast of having walked three miles across the sea. His private estates he sold at auction; he levied unheard of taxes; and scrupled not at open robbery, extortion, or other means however infamous so long as they brought him money. Yet he caused himself to be worshipped as a god, and it was this probably more than all else that led to his assassination. Matters were somewhat better in the reign of Claudius, who distributing large donations among the praetorian cohorts, introduced what became a regular custom at the accession of the emperors. Among his many public works were completed some from plans before regarded as impracticable, especially the famous aqueduct which bears his name.

In the year 64 A.D., the tenth of Nero's reign, occurred the great fire which, beginning in the wooden booths adjoining the Circus Maximus, swept over the city, until

NERO

after several days, its course was finally stayed by the Tiber and by the Servian wall. Of the fourteen districts into which Rome was divided, three were entirely obliterated, and of seven others little remained but the lurid skeletons of palace and temple walls. Four of the quarters survived; but of the most splendid of Roman mansions, of the most sacred of Roman fanes, of the trophies of Roman wars, and the monuments of Grecian art, nearly all were lost in the common destruction. By most authorities the conflagration was ascribed to Nero himself; but by Tacitus, whose verdict is probably worth all the rest, the emperor is acquitted of the crime, and certain it is that his prompt and energetic measures for the relief of the sufferers do not consist with this charge of wholesale incendiarism. In the imperial gardens and the Campus Martius was afforded shelter for the homeless, while provisions were sold at extremely low rates and among the destitute distributed free of charge. The reconstruction of the city was at once begun, and no precautions were spared that might avert the recurrence of such a catastrophe. The buildings were mainly of stone, of limited height, and separated by open spaces, while narrow and tortuous alleys and lanes gave place to wide and regular streets, the new city arising in greater splendor than ever before, as is often the case with centres of wealth overtaken by similar disasters.

While the value of monuments and gems of art and architecture cannot be estimated in sesterces, the loss in money and the cost of rebuilding were probably larger than at any of the great conflagrations which have occurred before or since. More costly than all was the "golden house" which Nero erected as his palace, its walls adorned with masterpieces of Grecian art and ablaze with precious metals and precious stones; its grounds laid out in meadows, groves, and lakes, beyond which appeared in perspective some of the finest views near the city of the seven hills. Of all the emperor's iniquities and extravagances none gave so much offence as the building of this mammoth edifice, of the dimension of which it need only be said that the Colosseum and the thermae of Titus later occupied only a small portion of its site. That it obstructed the public thoroughfare, and that to make room for it were demolished hundreds of buildings that had escaped destruction in one of the populous quarters of Rome, was to Nero a matter of no significance. It gratified his vanity, as also did the colossal bronze statue of himself which stood in one of the porticos. To defray the expense, says Tacitus, Italy and many of the provinces were ransacked, thus adding to the discontent in Rome the hatred of those who were now the mainstay of the empire. After masquerading in Greece as a competitor in the arena and a worshipper of Hellenic art, neglecting meanwhile the affairs of the nation, sentence of death being pronounced against him by the senate, Nero took his own life to escape the public executioner, and with him ended the line of the Caesars, though the title was still retained. His statues were broken or defaced; his golden house was destroyed, and from all Roman and other monuments his name was erased.

Passing over the reigns of Galba, Otho, and Vitellius, we come to that of Vespasian, the first of the Flavian emperors but a man of humble origin, his father being a tax-gatherer and money-lender. Proving himself an able leader, he was proclaimed by a majority of the legions; for by the legions, after the death of Nero, emperors were made and unmade, the sanction of the senate being merely a matter of form. It was largely during his reign that Rome was rebuilt, including its Colosseum, its temple of Capitoline Jove, its temple of Peace, and its public library. The avarice with which he was charged by Tacitus and Suetonius would appear rather to have been a studied system of economy, absolutely necessary in the disorganized condition of Roman finances. On occasion he could be

VESPASIAN

liberal enough, and many were the impoverished nobles and senators, the professors and men of letters on whom he bestowed pensions of several hundred thousand sesterces a year. Of his son and successor Titus it is said that he devoted nearly all his private fortune to the relief of those left homeless and destitute by the disaster which in 79 befell Herculaneum and Pompeii.

By Nerva were remedied, so far as possible, the evils committed by his predecessor Domitian, especially in the recall of exiles and relief from excessive taxation. Trajan, the fourteenth Roman emperor, was the first who was not an Italian by birth, though probably of Italian parentage. He was a thorough soldier, had seen hard service before assuming the purple, and was loved and respected by the legions; so that

TRAJAN

his election was readily confirmed throughout the empire. Entering Rome on foot some two years later, he gained at once the affections of the senate and people; for he lived among the latter as simply as he had lived among his soldiers, sharing their simple rations of bread and cheese, of salt pork and sour wine. For himself he discarded both power and pomp, proclaiming himself merely a citizen ruler, not above but subject to the laws. Presenting his sword to the commander of the praetorian guards, he exclaimed; "Use it for me if I do well, but against me if I do ill." His distributions of food and money were on a liberal scale, as also were his public works, and especially the fortifications which strengthened the great lines of defence between the Danube and the Nile. Returning in 106 laden with treasure from his Dacian campaigns, his triumph was of surpassing splendor, the games lasting four months as was said, while 10,000 beasts and almost as many gladiators contended in the arena.

HADRIAN, BERLIN MUSEUM

To Hadrian the provinces were more his care than the imperial city itself, though in the latter he distributed large donations, remitting also the arrears of taxes for many years. None knew better than he that the time for conquest was over; that the limits of the empire as established by Augustus were not only ample in extent, but presented a frontier which could be readily defended, and that the aim should no longer be to enlarge but to consolidate and improve the condition of the regions already won. Hence his tours of the provinces accompanied by corps of architects and artisans, lasting for fifteen years and including all portions of his dominions. Everywhere in the shape of temples, aqueducts, fotresses or other public works he left the impress of his energy and liberality, and especially did he favor Athens, adding to it an entire quarter and completing the temple of the Olympian Zeus.

MARCUS AURELIUS

Of Antoninus Pius, adopted son and successor of Hadrian, it is related that instead of despoiling the provinces to minister to Roman luxury, he expended his private fortune in aiding the provinces. Living with his destined heir, Marcus Aurelius, most of their time was passed in the seaside villa of Laurium, the birthplace of Antoninus, where far from the vices and intrigues of Rome their lives were passed in study and in the simplest of pleasures and occupations. Aurelius has been called the crown and flower of Stoicism, and in his instruction was engaged such a body of teachers as for acquirements and character had never before been assembled even in Rome, where the most accomplished of Greek professors could be hired for 200 sesterces a year. During his reign occurred a series of disasters, flood famine and earthquake, fire and pestilence following in quick succession, while revolts were frequent and in several quarters the empire was threatened by barbarian hordes. The brief intervals between his wars he devoted to study, the fruits of which are read to-day with even greater interest than the works of the classic masters. His *Meditations* come nearer to the teachings of the New Testament than those of any of the non-Christian philosophers, and yet, though the avowed apostle of moderation and temperance, he sanctioned a most cruel persecution of the Christians. They were written in the midst of public affairs, or perhaps on the eve of battles on which hung the fate of the empire, thus giving to them a fragmentary character, which does not, however, detract from their merit and charm. As some would have us believe, they were intended only for the use

of his son Commodus; but if so they signally failed of their purpose; for of all the tyrants who wore the purple there were none more degraded than Commodus. The friends of his father were butchered merely because they were wealthy, learned, or men of honor and probity. As for himself he fairly wallowed in vice; maintaining three hundred concubines, indulging in the most shameless debaucheries, appearing as a gladiator in the circus, and associating with buffoons, of whom he was himself the chief.

COMMODUS

From the days of Commodus the annals of Rome contain little more than a succession of wars and intrigues, of deeds of tyranny and baseness, of pitiful exhibitions of impotence and folly, and disgusting exhibitions of brutality and vice, such as even Gibbon tires of describing. Here and there was a special monster of wickedness like Caracalla, and there were some whose qualities shed lustre for a time on the decadence of the empire; such men as Septimius Severus, Probus, and Constantine the Great. But it

was only with the utmost difficulty that the vast fabric of imperial Rome was preserved from dissolution. In addition to foreign wars there was a series of desperate struggles between rival aspirants to the purple, more than a score of emperors who sat in the seat of Augustus during the third century meeting with a violent death, six of them almost within as many months.

SEPTIMUS SEVERUS

The weakness of the central authority was further increased by the establishment of provincial empires, first in Gaul under Postumus, and later in the East. The Syrian governor Odaenathus, for instance, prince of Palmyra, assumed the independent sovereignty of many eastern provinces, and his titles and possessions were inherited by his son, though the real power was in the hands of his widow Zenobia, who declaring herself empress openly defied the power of Rome. After a hard-fought campaign won more by gold than strategy, Palmyra was taken in 272, and its queen led captive to adorn the triumph of Aurelian. The spoils were enormous; for Palmyra was now the mistress of the eastern world, the emporium of the rich traffic of India, China, and Arabia, Rome herself importing yearly her jewels and pearls, her silks and other

CARACALLA

ZENOBIA

costly fabrics to the value of hundreds of millions of sesterces. The city itself was spared; but only to be destroyed and its inhabitants massacred after the revolt of the following year.

It was during the third century that successive hordes of barbarians and semi-barbarians began to lay waste the provinces, crippling their resources and inflicting on their inhabitants the scourges of famine and pestilence. In the east were the Parthians, and in the north the Goths the Franks and Alemanni, all making the best use of the opportunities afforded by internal dissension and strife. After defeating the emperor Decius, the Goths compelled his successor Gallus to purchase peace by costly gifts, and a few years later, with a fleet of 500 sail, ravaged the coasts of Greece and Asia Minor, returning with the spoils of Athens, Argos, and Corinth.

In the reign of Diocletian, who associated with himself Maximian, and later among several others Constantius and Galerius, the empire was reorganized under a system which,

DIOCLETIAN

without the sacrifice of unity, distributed among them the cares and responsibilities of government. The armies were also divided, each having its own imperator, and with this change disappeared the last traces of the republican and Augustan eras, with their limited powers and definite prerogatives. Despotism, open and undisguised, was further hedged about with the pomp and formalities of oriental royalty, as in the wearing of the diadem, of silk and golden garments, and in the genuflexions and prostrations which succeeded the former method of salutation. Finally Rome was reduced to a level with the provinces, and for the first time since the founding of the eternal city Roman citizenship ceased to be a privilege.

For a brief period under the reign of Constantine the empire was again united, though the building of the new capital of Byzantium, with a separate senate and government, prepared the way for its final division under the rule of Valentinian. After the death of Theodosius in 395 came further barbaric invasions, Alaric the Visigoth laying siege to the city a few years later, but retiring under promise of a ransom of 5,000 pounds of gold and 30,000 of silver. Returning in 410, he entered Rome by night, and for six days handed it over to pillage, with all the attendant horrors. Vast as were the treasures secured, they were to him of little benefit; for in the same year they were buried with him in the bed of a river whose channel was diverted for the purpose, the captives employed on the work being put to death that none might know of their whereabouts. About the middle of the fifth century Attila, "the scourge of God," forces the Romans to purchase peace by the payment of a heavy tribute. As king of the Huns and other tribes north of the Danube and the Black sea, he was monarch of a mighty empire in northern and central Europe, defeating the Roman legions, laying waste the country around Byzantium, and dictating terms to the emperors of the east and west. In Gaul he appears in 451 with an army 700,000 strong, and though at first successful, is finally defeated at Chalons after one of the most desperate conflicts recorded in history. In the following summer he ravages northern Italy; but when Rome appeared to be in his grasp is induced to retire by an embassy from the supreme pontiff. Three years later comes the storming of the city by Genseric, king of the Vandals, followed by fourteen days and nights of pillage and plunder, with the violation of matrons and maids whose chastity, nevertheless, the church declares inviolate. Among the spoils was nearly all that remained of public or private wealth, of treasures sacred or profane, including temple ornaments, and even the appendages of Jewish worship which Titus brought from Jerusalem, the golden table and the golden candlestick with seven branches, deposited in the temple of Peace. The ornaments of the imperial palaces, with their costly furniture and wardrobes, their massive gold and silver plate, their jewelry and precious stones also contributed to the booty, whose total value amounted to several thousands of talents. Finally, in 476 A.D. Romulus Augustulus is deposed in favor of Odoacer the

Rugian, and a barbarian monarch is seated on the throne of the Caesars.

As to the Rome of the middle ages little is known; for endless wars with their attendant pillagings and conflagrations left but few original documents on which to base the annals of the state. After the partition of the empire its western capital gradually became the religious rather than the political centre of the world, though the bestowal of rich estates and benefices by the supreme pontiffs infused new blood into the aristocracy and gave to it at least a semblance of vitality. Many of the pontiffs were wealthy, and not a few were men of marked ability, possessing more worldly power than any European sovereign. Such a man, for example, was Gregory I, who administered with the greatest prudence the vast possessions and revenues of the church; so that the army being unpaid when the city was besieged by the Lombards, he supplied the funds first for the defence and then for the ransom of the city. Later the authority of the popes, after many struggles with Italian nobles and foreign potentates, was acknowledged even in matters temporal, almost throughout the civilized world.

The building of churches began in Rome during the reign of Constantine, before whose time the Christians must worship in their own houses or meet by stealth in the catacombs. Their earlier sanctuaries, of which those that remain have been altered beyond recognition, were of simple construction, rectangular in shape with walls of concrete faced with brick, and plain windows of glass or translucent alabaster. In the interior were sculptured marble shafts of many designs, and in not a few were columns taken from the classic structures of the capitol. It was not until the fourteenth century that the erection of the papal palaces was begun, though before that date there were many beautiful compositions in marble enriched with mosaics, especially in the form of altars, tombs, and campaniles. The Lateran palace, of the original of which, built in the age of Nero and at least thrice as large as the present structure, the Capella Sancta Sanctorum is all that remains, was the favorite residence of the popes. Its present use, as rebuilt by order of Sixtus V nearly three centuries after its destruction by fire, is for a museum of classic sculpture and Christian antiquities.

The Vatican palace as it now exists, the largest in the world, and the abode of the pontiffs after their return from Avignon, was begun by Nicholas V in 1447, its enlargement, completion, and decoration being due to several of the pontiffs, of whom Pius IX gave to it the finishing touches and supplied its grand flight of stairs. It has twenty courts, hundreds of halls, salas, chapels, and thousands of apartments, only a few of which are devoted to the papal court. Here amid a vast assortment of Roman and

VATICAN GALLERY

Graeco-Roman statuary are gems of pure Hellenic art, with a valuable collection of Greek vases and relics from Etruscan tombs. In the library, with its 27,000 Latin, Greek, and oriental manuscripts, its archives of the middle ages, its correspondence of the pontiffs, and registers of papal acts from the days of Innocent III, are beautiful specimens of mediaeval art-work in the form of plate and jewels. A picture gallery of moderate size is stored with works of more than average merit, among which are canvases by several of the great masters. On the ceiling of the Sistine chapel is some of the finest workmanship of Michael

VATICAN LIBRARY

Angelo, and on the altar wall, blackened by the smoke of centuries, is his famous painting of 'The Last Judgment.'

The original church of St. Peter is said to have been founded by Constantine on the site of Nero's circus, where the apostle suffered martyrdom. It was in the form of a basilica, with nave, transept, and double aisles divided by Corinthian colonnades, its apse, in the central curve of which was the pontifical chair, being screened by pillars of Parian marble taken, as was claimed, from Solomon's temple. While the interior was profusely decorated with gold and mosaic work, it was externally less imposing than other Roman basilicas, especially those of Trajan and Maxentius, the latter usually known as the temple of Peace.

For the present cathedral of St. Peter the plans were drawn by Bramante, the greatest architect of the Florentine period, in the form of a Greek cross covered with a gigantic dome resembling that of the Pantheon. The foundation stone was laid in 1506; but after his death, a few years later, Bramante's design was discarded, the completion of the work being intrusted to Raphael, Michael Angelo and others. In 1626 the building was consecrated by Urban VIII, costing with additions since that date, including the sacristy erected by Pius VI, more than $50,000,000. In size it is nearly twice as large as the cathedrals of Milan and St. Paul, covering nearly four acres of ground, 640 feet in length and 435 in height from the pavement to the summit of the cross, which surmounts a dome 630 feet in circumference. The portico, flanked with equestrian statues of Charlemagne and Constantine, is handsomely decorated, and at the entrances are antique columns of African marble, with other embellishments in doubtful taste, especially in the panels representing Christian subjects bordered with scenes from classic mythology, as the rape of Europa by Jupiter in the form of a bull. While to the exterior

BASILICA OF ST. LORENZO

exception may be taken, the internal effect is extremely impressive, the enormous dome with the arcades below, the great dome pillars, and the arms of the cross forming the most striking features of an architectural composition the vastness of which is concealed by harmony of proportion.

During the latter part of the fifteenth and the opening years of the sixteenth century Rome was enriched with many stately and beautiful structures, for the most part of

Florentine architecture. Among them were the Palazzo di Venezia of Paul II, built as were others of travertine blocks from the Colosseum; the Palazzo della Cancelleria, one of Bramante's masterpieces, as also were the adjoining church of Saint Lorenzo in Damaso, and the Palazzo Giraud, the former residence of Cardinal Wolsey and of Raphael. By Raphael were designed the Palazzo Vidoni, where in 1536 Charles was entertained as the guest of the Caffarelli, and the Palazzo Madama, the former residence of the grand-dukes of Tuscany and now the meeting-place of the Italian senate. The Palazzo Farnese, where are the quarters of the French embassy to the papal court, was designed in part by Michael Angelo, and ranks among the

FARNESE PALACE

finest compositions of the renaissance. The small but exceedingly tasteful structure known as the Villa Farnesina was completed in 1511 for the banker of the supreme pontiffs, later passing by inheritance to Cardinal Farnese and his family, and thence to the king of Naples. On the ceiling of the entrance hall are illustrations of the myth of Psyche, designed by Raphael, and in an adjoining chamber is another mythological study entirely of his own composition — Galatea crossing the sea in a shell, surrounded with cupids nymphs and tritons.

CAPITOLINE MUSEUM

With museums and art galleries, both public and private, Rome is plentifully supplied. In the Capitoline museum is a valuable collection of classic statuary bronzes and coins. In the Museo Kircheriano, founded in 1601 by the Jesuit teacher after whom it was named, are grouped among other antiquities most of the prehistoric specimens in stone and iron, pottery and bronze, discovered in Italy and the islands adjacent. The university of Rome has its geological cabinets, together with a large assortment of minerals, and of the marbles used in the building of the ancient city. In the Borghese, Corsini, Doria, and Barberini palaces are the most famous of private art galleries, though except for the first containing little above the level of mediocrity. In the Barberini library are several thousand manuscripts, many of them by Greek and Latin authors, and of public libraries the largest is the Biblioteca Vittorio Emanuele, with more than half a million volumes and manuscripts, to which additions are constantly made from the choicest of current literature.

Of other Italian cities mention must be of the briefest; for that Paris is France is not more true than that Italy is merged in the eternal city. Yet the population of Rome is far exceeded by that of Naples, the most densely peopled, and as to site the most beautiful of European capitals. Though originally a Greek settlement, there are many traces of Roman occupation, as in the tunnel constructed probably about 30 B.C. through the promontory of Posillipo, 2,200 feet in length and in places 70 in height. Long before that date it had become a Roman possession, and in the days of Cicero was a centre of wealth and culture, though its inhabitants were noted, as today they are, for their indolent and effeminate habits. During the empire it was a favorite resort not only for the rich but for the emperors themselves, and it was here that Nero made his first appearance on the stage. In the Gothic and other wars, and especially from the Lombards, it suffered many disasters and many changes of government, enjoying but the briefest intervals of peace, until in 1861 it was absorbed in the kingdom of Italy, of which it is to-day, as under Roman rule, one of the most beautiful and opulent cities.

The buildings of modern Naples are more remarkable for size than taste, most of them five or more stories in height, flat-roofed, stucco covered, and flanking narrow but well-paved streets. In former ages the city was protected by the castle of St. Elmo, built in the fourteenth century by Robert the Wise, and reconstructed in the sixteenth by Charles V, with massive ramparts and fosses hewn through the solid rock. Rich in mediaeval sculpture is the church San Domenico Maggiore, adjacent to which is the convent that contains the cell of Thomas Aquinas. Many of the Neapolitan churches and Convents have been converted into museums, among them the Carthusian monastery, a richly decorated edifice with works of art by Guido, Ribera, and other masters.

NAPLES

The national museum, commonly termed the Museo Borbonico, is a storehouse of Roman and Italian antiquities, including the Farnese collection, and all that was best worth preserving from the ruins of Pompeii, Herculaneum, Paestum, and other ancient cities. The Biblioteca Nazionale is the largest of Neapolitan libraries, containing some 400,000 volumes and 10,000 manuscripts, among them the collection of Cardinal Seripando and other valuable acquisitions of rare and curious works. The university of Naples, founded in 1224 by Frederick II, is the oldest in Italy, except those of Bologna and Padua, its muster-roll containing the names of more than 5,000 students. Among other institutions are the Royal society of Naples, the Royal college of music, and the Zoological station, one of the leading centres of modern research. Charitable establishments are numerous and

NAPLES MUSEUM

handsomely endowed; the principal hospital has an income of $160,000 a year and accommodates 1,000 patients; the almshouse with its fine range of buildings has an annual revenue of $250,000. There are at least a score of theatres, of which the San Carlo opera-house is the largest in the world. It is liberally subsidized, and with it are intimately associated the names of Rossini, Donizetti, and others of the great composers.

On the bay of Naples and the gulf adjacent are several towns and villages whose sites are among the most beautiful in Europe, as Sorrento with its historic memories, Amalfi, once the capital of a great mediaeval republic, and Salerno with its white terraced houses, its half-ruined Lombard castle, and its ancient cathedral, where Pope Hildebrand and Margaret of Anjou lie at rest.

But for the dramatic interest connected with its destruction, and for the discoveries brought to light by modern excavations, Pompeii, with its world-wide repute, would have been known, if known at all, merely as a provincial town. Toward the close of the republican era, however, and during the earlier empire it had become a favorite seaside resort for wealthy Romans, many of whom had here their villas, Cicero, for instance, speaking with affection of his Pompeiian residence. In 63 A.D. it was partially destroyed

STREET OF THE SEPULCHRES, POMPEII

by earthquake, and the inhabitants were still engaged in rebuilding their shattered edifices when overtaken by the catastrophe which a few years later buried the place beneath the ashes of Vesuvius. While by the same eruption Herculaneum was entombed under a solid mass of lava, Pompeii was covered only with scoriae and fragments of volcanic rock; but to a depth of fifteen or twenty feet, thus obliterating all traces of its buildings and streets, so that for nearly sixteen centuries even its site remained unknown.

As reproduced through explorations beginning as far back as 1755, the town was well laid out, with straight and well paved streets intersecting at right angles, but seldom more than 20 and never more than 30 feet in width. As in Rome, and nearly all Roman

DOMESTIC UTENSILS, POMPEII

towns, the forum was the centre of business activity and the resort of the lounger and politician. It was an elegant rather than an imposing structure, with a series of porticos on three of its sides, some of them arcaded and others supported on columns. Around it were the public buildings, the temples, the basilicas, the thermae, the theatres, and not far away an amphitheatre used for gladiatorial show; but neither in their design nor materials is there anything to indicate that Pompeii ranked higher than a second or third-class provincial town. As to works of art, while there are statuettes of finished and beautiful workmanship, the larger

statues, both in marble and bronze, are surpassed by those of Herculaneum. In the paintings also there is little to commend from an artistic point of view, though many are valuable as illustrations of the lives and habits of the people.

Milan, almost in the centre of the rich plain of Lombardy, is enclosed with a wall seven miles in circuit, within which are the homes of 450,000 people. The cathedral, begun in 1386, is the work of several centuries and of many architects; the finishing touches were

given, it is said, under the instructions of Napoleon in 1805. In size it is one of the largest in the world, 480 feet in length by 180 in width, with a tower 360 feet in height. It is of cruciform shape and of Gothic design, though with features of the Romanesque. The walls are cased in marble, and of white marble is the roof, supported on 50 pillars, with niches for statuary, of which there are in all 2,000 pieces. A more ancient church is the one named after its founder Saint Ambrose, and erected in the fourth century on the ruins of a temple of Dionysius. Among other structures worthy of note are the royal and archiepiscopal

MILAN CATHEDRAL

palaces, the town-hall erected early in the fifteenth century, the Great hospital completed a few years later, and the Scala theatre, one of the finest in Italy. As the former home of many celebrated painters, sculptors, and architects, Milan is rich in works of art. World-famous is the picture gallery of the Brera, with its studies by Raphael, by Paul Veronese and others of the Venetian school, while in the Brera library are 250,000 volumes and a collection of manuscripts second only to that of the Biblioteca Ambrosiana.

Turin, though at least as ancient as the days of Hannibal, by whom it was captured 218 B.C., is in appearance one of most modern of Italian cities, with spacious squares and wide and regular streets. Its cathedral of St. John the Baptist is of fifteenth century renaissance architecture, and behind its high altar is the chapel of the Sudario, the shroud with which Joseph of Arimathea is said to have covered the body of Christ. In the tower of the church of La Beata Vergine are Vela's famous statues of Maria Theresa and Maria

CATHEDRAL, FLORENCE

Adelaide. The Madama palace, built as first it stood by William of Montferrat, and the royal palace, with its museum of mineralogy and zoology, are the finest of the secular buildings. In the Castello palace is a valuable collection of manuscripts and drawings, including sketches by Raphael and Michael Angelo.

Of Florence the first mention is in connection with the ancient Etruscan town of Faesulae, of which it was probably a suburb, attaining the rank of city after its colonization by Sulla. In the fifteenth century it had become one of the leading centres of wealth, as now it is of literature and art, its treasures ranking second only to those of the capital. Of its three large libraries the Nazionale, with its half million of volumes, is noted for its size, the Marucelliana for its drawings and works on art, and the Laurentian, of which Lorenzo de Medici was the founder, for its

UFFIZI GALLERY, FLORENCE

manuscripts and illuminated missals. Of Florentian galleries of art, as of the Pitti and Uffizi, with their masterpieces by Titian and Raphael, it is unnecessary here to speak; for their art, like their architecture is known to all the world. Palaces are numerous in Florence,

GENOA

as those of the Corsi, the Corsini, and the Strozi; but more interesting perhaps than all are the former homes of Dante, Machiavelli, and others whose classic works belong not to Italy alone but to the world.

Genoa, like Turin, played its part in the second Punic war, thereafter passing through many tribulations before it became worthy of its title of the Superb. It is a city of palaces, of elaborate and somewhat florid architecture, oldest among which, besides smaller ones, is the palace of the doges, now used by the prefecture, its adjacent tower and belfry dating from the fourteenth century. In the sixteenth century palace, erected for the dukes of Turin and later used for municipal purposes, are many curious relics, including the violin of Paganini and autograph letters by Columbus. To the same period belongs the palace of Victor Emanuel built originally for the Durazzos, the owners of many mansions. Of nearly a hundred churches the oldest is that of St. Ambrose and St. Peter, founded in the sixth century and restored by the Jesuits more than a thousand years later. Among its art treasures are Guido Reni's 'Assumption' and Rubens' 'Circumcision' and 'St. lgnatius.' The cathedral of St. Lawrence was in the ninth century of metropolitan rank, though nothing remains of the original structure, the present building and its decorations being the work of many artists and artificers. Especially rich in columnar ornaments, in statuary and arabesques is its chapel of St. John the Baptist, where women may enter only once a year; for was he not the victim of a woman's malice? Museums, libraries, and institutions of learning are plentiful, a palace in the Via Balbi being set apart for the royal university; and nowhere in Italy are benevolent associations more richly endowed, the duke of Galliera alone donating or bequeathing in charities thirty millions of francs.

It was not until early in the ninth century that any permanent settlement was made on the site of Venice, and for two or three centuries thereafter it consisted merely of a

CANAL IN VENICE

number of cabins clustered among the grassy islets that skirt the Venetian coast. Fishing was the chief occupation of the inhabitants; but presently came commerce and with commerce wealth; so that in the thirteenth century they had become the richest and most powerful community in the world, with large possessions on the mainland of Europe.

Modern Venice is built on 117 islands connected by the 400 bridges which span its 150 canals. Recent improvements have somewhat marred its beauty, especially the iron bridges across the Grand canal, and the so-called omnibus steamers and clumsy, dark-cabined gondolas that have taken the place of the sightly craft of former days, with their awnings of gold embroideries. In population it ranks eighth among Italian cities, with more than 150,000 inhabitants, and a considerable volume of commerce and manufactures, the latter remaining almost as they were in the middle ages, when from the Arabs they borrowed the decorative arts and from the Persians the art of weaving costly tissues.

Of other Italian cities, as Verona, with its cathedral, and Pisa, with its tower, it is unnecessary here to make other than passing mention. To a certain class of people a more

LEANING TOWER, PISA

interesting spot than any is Monaco, the smallest and probably the most densely populated of European principalities, nearly 15,000 people living on its eight square miles of territory. It has long been a resort for invalids as well as for gamesters, and nowhere on the Franco-Italian shore is there a more beautiful climate or a more sheltered coast. The first gambling saloon was here established in 1856, and later passed into the hands of a joint-stock company with a capital of $3,000,000. Monte Carlo gaming tables began to be fashionable in 1860, under the management of M. Blanc, a refugee from Homburg, and the casino afterward erected was never in want of patrons.

While Italy is essentially an agricultural country, manufactures are on a considerable scale. As a silk-producing region it ranks second only to China, and next in order are cottons, chiefly in the form of coarse fabrics, while the weaving of flax and hemp, mainly by hand-looms, gives employment to 70,000 operatives. In the production of packing, blotting, and other papers are used more than 50,000 tons a year of linen rags. Of leather the annual output is valued at $25,000,000; the manufacture of iron and light machinery are thriving industries, and among articles of minor importance are sugar, oils, and liquors. The ceramic arts, for which Italy was famous a century ago, have fallen into decadence; but jewelry and trinkets, fashioned principally in Rome, are largely exported or purchased by tourists, while Roman. Florentine, and Venetian mosaics are also in general favor.

Agriculture is for the most part in a primitive condition, with implements so far behind the age that the Roman plough described by Virgil is still in use. Cereals are raised in nearly all the provinces, and especially in the plain of Lombardy; but for many other

products the available area is limited by climatic conditions. Thus the coast lands around Genoa, between the Apennines and the sea, are among the most favored spots for olives and citrus fruits, neither of which can be raised in the region north of the mountains, where in places the winter climate is colder than that of Denmark. And so with central Italy, in whose upland valleys entire communities are debarred by heavy snowstorms from all communication with their neighbors. Yet

OLIVE WOODS

almost within sight of them are districts where the orange and fig-tree thrive luxuriantly on the borders of the Adriatic. In Calabria the contrast is especially marked; sub-tropical fruits, the sugar-cane, and cotton-plant ripening to perfection on its shores, a few miles from which are ranges covered with the fir and pine. In southern Italy the climate resembles that of Greece, except for the malaria which has given over to desolation many

WINE-MAKING

of the fertile plains encircled in former ages by a girdle of opulent settlements. The vine is cultivated almost throughout the peninsula, the production of wine exceeding 500,000,000 gallons a year, most of it for local consumption. As market gardeners the Italians have no superiors, earning a fair livelihood in the neighborhood of cities on lands for which they pay a rental of $100 an acre. The supply of live-stock is sufficient to permit a considerable export, and the forestry department adds nearly $20,000,000 a year to the revenue of the state, the total value of all agricultural and forest products exceeding $1,200,000,000 a year. Of minerals sulphur and zinc are the most important, while the yield of the marble and other quarries is valued at $5,000,000 a year.

Since the unification of the Italian kingdom under Victor Emanuel, to whom his eldest son Humbert has proved no unworthy successor, the commerce of Italy has been largely developed, especially with the neighboring countries of Switzerland and France. For 1894 the total exports were estimated at $225,000,000, with imports of somewhat larger amount. Of the former, silk is the principal item, and next are wines, fruits, olive-oil, and provisions in various forms. Grain, raw cotton, and coal are the principal imports, foreign cereals to the amount of some $30,000,000 a year being required for the consumption of a people whose diet consists almost entirely of bread and thin rice soup. With her large extent of coast, her abundance of excellent harbors, her central position on the Mediterranean seaboard, and the

VICTOR EMANUEL

advantage of railroad communication with transalpine countries, it is probable that Italy will erelong attain to the commercial position from which she has been debarred by many cycles of political disturbance.

Sicily, the wealthiest and most important of the Mediterranean islands, was for several centuries dominated by the Greeks, though subject at intervals to Carthaginian encroachments, the native tribes, named Sikanoi, and the Sikeloi, originally an Italian race, which first appeared in Sicily about 1100 B.C., being finally absorbed in the Hellenic settlements. During the seventh and sixth centuries these settlements became the most prosperous of the Grecian colonies, rivalling even Athens and Corinth in wealth and the luxuries that wealth can purchase, while in architectural monuments and works of art they were not greatly their inferiors. The reign of the tyrants, beginning with that of Phalaris of Agrigentum, whose holocaust of the brazen bull is probably a Phoenician tradition, was in the main beneficial, for most of them were tyrants only in name and rather the champions than the oppressors of their country. The praises of Hieron, for instance, were sung by Pindar, and Dionysius, his wars at an end, devoted himself to the planting of colonies.

In the Persian and Peloponnesian wars the nation suffered but little, though playing an important part in both, especially at the siege of Syracuse, where the destruction of the fleet and army of Nicias, on which Athens had expended the last talent in her treasury, gave the death-blow to Athenian supremacy. During the first Punic war many cities were pillaged by the contending parties, Sicily becoming first an ally and then a province of

Rome. It was frequently plundered during the later republic by Roman governors, and especially by Verres, who after bringing desolation on a contented and prosperous people, stripping them of their most valuable possessions, including treasures of art beyond all price, boasted that he had enough to maintain him in ease and luxury, though he should bribe a Roman jury with two-thirds of his spoils. A few centuries later the country became subject to Genseric the Vandal, and then in turn to the Goths, the Byzantine emperors, the Saracens, the Normans, the Lombards, and others, finally, after many changes of dynasty, becoming a portion of the kingdom of Italy.

Syracuse, founded only a score of years after the founding of Rome, played an imperial part in the classic annals of Sicily. In the fifth century its citizens had become an exclusive and aristocratic body, owning large tracts of valuable land, this element developing first into a tyranny and then into a democracy, though whatever the form of government, the city increased in wealth and power until it passed under Roman rule. In

ARCHIMEDES

212 B.C. it surrendered, after an obstinate defence, to Marcellus, who carried away its treasures of art and handed it over to pillage, Archimedes being one of those who lost their lives in the massacre which followed. Later it again became a stately and opulent city, with temples, amphitheatres and other public buildings, some of them erected or restored by Caligula. In modern Syracuse there is little of interest except its cathedral, erected on the site of an ancient fane of Minerva. Of Agrigentum, once the centre of Sicilian commerce, luxury, and wealth, nothing but its ruins remain. More even than Syracuse it was noted for its splendid architectural monuments, the remnants of which, especially those of the temple of Olympian Jove, attest its former greatness.

Most of the surface of Sicily lies several hundred feet above the sea, with mountain ranges several thousand feet in height, and above all the volcano of Etna, rising nearly 11,000 feet from its 400 square miles of base. In some of the valleys, plains, and plateaus there is an abundant yield of cereals and fruits, oranges and olives, of which there are continuous groves on the northern mountain slopes, being largely raised for export. Wheat is still the leading product of the country, as in the days of the Roman empire, of which it was the principal granary. Commerce is of small amount; manufactures are few and unimportant, and as to minerals, sulphur, the deposits of which are estimated at 5,00,000,000, is the only one of economic value.

In minerals Sardinia is the richest of the Italian provinces, its mines being worked by the Carthaginians and Romans, while there are probably at least a hundred in operation at the present day, most of them in the province of Iglesias. Silver and argentiferous lead, zinc, and iron are worked with fair returns; there are also copper, antimony, arsenic, nickel, cobalt, and of coal an abundant supply, though as yet but little utilized. Agriculture is in a backward condition, due rather to malaria than to lack of fertility; for in former ages Sardinia was second only to Sicily among the granaries of Rome. There are no manufactures worthy of the name; but commerce is steadily increasing, showing almost a three-fold gain within the last quarter of a century. Sassari is the largest town, and Cagliari, the capital, with its high-mounted castle, its viceregal palace, its cathedral, university, and mansions of the noble and wealthy is the principal seaport and railroad terminus. Here and elsewhere on the island are many remains of the period when Sardinia was a Carthaginian colony, and in the tombs have been discovered strong traces of Egyptian settlements.

Malta, though a British possession, belongs geographically to Italy. The island contains a large number of historic ruins of great interest, as the stone erections in Gozo, the great temple of Melkart, and the excavations of Hagiar Kim. The manufactures and commerce which attained great importance under the Phoenicians, continued through the Augustan age of Rome, The Knights of Malta received large sums from a grateful Christendom for the advancement of Valetta, "a city erected by gentlemen for gentlemen"

HARBOR OF VALETTA, MALTA

as they termed it. The modern town is built along and across a ridge of rock, its streets ending toward the harbor in flights of stairs, and bordered with flat-roofed houses, many of them with covered balconies projecting from the windows, giving to the place a strong element of the picturesque.

PONTE VECCHIO, FLORENCE

41

MISCELLANY. — Except for the remains of Roma Quadrata, the Tullianum is probably the most ancient monument of the regal period. As its name implies, its first use was probably as a cistern, the word tullius signifying a spring of water. Later it was converted into a dungeon — the barathron of Plutarch and the Mamertine prison of the middle ages. Into its loathsome cells, through a hole in the stone floor above, its only aperture, Jugurtha, the Catiline conspirators, and other political offenders were lowered, some to be strangled and some to be starved to death. It has been said that St. Peter and St. Paul here suffered imprisonment.

Among the most striking specimens of Cyclopean architecture are the walls of the town of Norba on a declivity overlooking the Pontine marshes. The town was burned to the ground by Sulla, but the walls are almost intact as also is the principal gate. Etruscan remains are numerous, and among them may be mentioned a conical mound called the Cucumella, 650 feet in circumference, where in a central crypt walled in with massive masonry, whose secret has never been disclosed, lie the remains of the Lucuno and his kin. On the summit were found the bases of crumbling towers, and in the cuttings winged sphynxes, lions, and other animals from which a restoration of the mysterious vault was possible.

To Servius Tullius is ascribed the introduction of coined money, its shape and standard of value probably borrowed from that of the Etruscans. The most ancient coin was the as, formed of the compound metal called aes, which may have been either brass or bronze, and named the as libralis from its weight of one liber or pound. At first the coins were oblong and afterward round in shape, the latter being stamped on one side with the double head of Janus and on the other with the prow of a ship. After the exhaustion of the treasury caused by the first Punic war the weight was reduced to two ounces, and in the reign of Severus to less than one-fifth of an ounce. The silver denarius was worth about 16 cents, and 25 of these were equal to a gold denarius. The sesterce was equal to somewhat less than five cents, and the sestertium, which represented 1,000 sesterces was a sum and not a coin. In the time of Augustus, while the precious metals circulated side by side, only silver was used for coinage, gold being paid and taken by weight.

It is more than probable that in the second Punic war Hannibal used gunpowder or some other form of explosive. Certain it is that Alpine rocks could not be eaten away with vinegar, as is the common story, and it is difficult to account for the overturning of huge masses of rock on the Roman legions in the defile skirting Lake Thrasimene, except by the use of explosives.

Maecenas, the patron of Horace and one of the wealthiest citizens of the Augustan era, was the first to erect public baths at his own expense. To ingratiate themselves with the people many of the emperors, and especially Nero, Titus, Domitian, Caracalla, and Diocletian constructed thermae of vast extent, containing not only baths and suites of bathing apartments, but gymnasia, theatres, and libraries. Among the various chambers were the apodyterium where the bathers stripped, the unctuarium where they were anointed, and the caledarium and frigidarium where were hot and cold baths, with others used for steam and plunge baths and for dressing rooms. In the thermae of Diocletian, it is said, were 3,200 marble seats, and in those of Caracalla 1,600, a hall in the former being converted into a church of spacious dimensions, while the latter were more than a mile in circuit. For young men there was a place for playing ball and a stadium resembling, though on a smaller scale, the one in the Circus Maximus, while for philosophers and men of

SENECA

letters there were open colonnades where they might discuss the news or read aloud their productions. In the more pretentious structures the walls were covered with mosaics in imitation of pictorial art; the galleries were lined with stately columns and with the choicest of statuary; in the chambers were the masterpieces of Phidias and Praxiteles, and from the mouths of lions, fashioned of polished silver, streams of water were poured into silver basins. "Such is the luxury of our times," remarks Seneca, "that we are not content if we do not tread on gems in our bathrooms."

Of Apicius, an epicure who lived in the time of Tiberius, it is related that when he found he had but $400,000 left, after spending $4,000,000 on the delicacies of his table, he straightway went forth and hanged himself lest he should not be able to gratify his appetite.

Bewailing the use of gold rings, and remarking that "the worst crime committed against mankind was by him who first put a ring on his finger," Pliny mentions that the earlier Romans wore only those which were made of brass, as a token of warlike prowess. Yet the statement that after the battle of Cannae Hannibal sent to Carthage three modii of golden rings shows that they were in common use during the second Punic war and probably not restricted to the knights. Before and during the empire plain gold rings gave place to such as were engraved with various devices and set with gems of brilliant lustre, "loading the fingers with entire revenues," as Pliny puts it.

Of Herodes Atticus, an Athenian citizen of the time of Nerva, when Greece was a Roman province, it is related that his father having discovered a vast amount of treasure buried beneath his house, he offered it to the emperor Nerva, to whom, according to law, it belonged as treasure trove. But the monarch refused to accept it, or any part of it, bidding Herodes use it as he saw fit. Still the Athenian insisted, stating that it was too much for one who was merely his subject, and that he knew not what use to make of it. "Abuse it then," said the emperor, "for it is your own." Most of it he devoted to public works and buildings, erecting in Athens a stadium of white marble 600 feet in length and large enough for the entire population of the city.

NERVA,
UFFIZI GALLERY

In Vespasian's temple of Peace were many of the choicest works of art, and from its site has been unearthed a large quantity of valuable antiquities. Here, says Dion Cassius, was the favorite meeting place for artists and men of letters, the temple, containing a library with many rare and costly works.

To Antinous, page to the emperor Hadrian, for whose sake, it is said, he sacrificed his life, most extravagant honors were paid. Cities ware named after him; temples and monuments were erected, and festivals held in his memory, while oracles delivered their responses in his name, and finally the youth was worshipped as a god. One good result of these absurdities was to impart a strong impulse to the sculptor's art in the effort to reproduce the deified page in idealized form. In the Capitol, the Vatican, the Louvre, and elsewhere are statues, busts, and bas-reliefs, with innumerable medals stamped with his effigy.

To Pacificus, archdeacon of Verona during the ninth century, is ascribed the invention of clocks, though in nowise resembling those in modern use. Among other ancient clocks or horologia was that which the sultan of Egypt presented to Frederick II in 1232, in which the celestial bodies, impelled by wheels and weights, pointed to the hour of day or night. One made by the abbot of St. Alban's, England, is said to have shown such astronomical phenomena as could not be illustrated by mechanism elsewhere in the world.

The casa Polo was one of the most notable palaces in Venice after Mark's famous journey to the orient during the thirteenth century. On returning from his travels, he had

MARCO POLO

many wonderful stories to tell, so wonderful indeed that to relate what he saw and heard the word millions was repeatedly used; millions of diamonds, millions of ducats, millions of islands and kingdoms and kings. Hence the wits of Venice gave him the nickname of Il Milione, and the place where his house stood was called the corte del Milioni; but some say the name was given because he was a millionaire. Ramusio tells us that on the return of Marco Polo to Venice his friends and family would not receive him, until with a sharp knife he ripped open the seams and welts of his old clothes, out of which fell rubies, emeralds, and other jewels, into which he had converted all his wealth on taking leave of the great khan — then they believed him.

It is estimated that on an average about $100,000,000 are annually expended in Italy by travellers, the majority of whom are citizens of England or the United States. At present the only means of local travel are omnibuses and horse-cars; but a concession was recently granted for the building of an electric line from the post-office to the principal railroad station.

One of the first acts of King Humbert's reign was to pay a portion of his father's debts, and this he did from his own private fortune, of which he contributed nearly $4,000,000. Humbert is one of the most economical of monarchs, though economy is forced upon him by the impoverished condition of his people, abolishing more than 160 offices of court in a single year.

KING HUMBERT

By Barrett Browning was established in Asolo, opposite the house in which his father sojourned, a lace school where girls are taught how to reproduce old patterns of Venetian lace.

The debt of the Italian kingdom amounts to $2,375,000, or nearly $80 per capita, an enormous burden for a country where farm and other laborers can barely earn enough to keep body and soul together, and in some of whose cities, as in Venice, more than one-fourth of the people are supported by charity. Taxes are extremely heavy, though somewhat reduced within recent years, the estimated revenue for 1894-5 being $336,000,000, and the expenditure $357,000,000. The debt of Italy is about 50 per cent more and the expenditure only 20 per cent less than that of the United States, with twice her population and probably ten times her wealth.

Italy has about 9,500 miles of railways, belonging mainly to the state, though in 1885 their working was transferred under a 60 years' lease to private companies. The telegraph system, with some 25,000 miles in operation, is a government monopoly.

In case of war more than 3,000,000 troops could be mustered into service; but only 270,000 are included in the regular army, the remainder consisting of mobile and territorial militia and men on unlimited leave. The navy ranks third among those of European powers, with 16 battle or port defence ships, 61 cruisers, and 150 torpedo boats.

CHAPTER THE EIGHTH

SPAIN, PORTUGAL

Riches are of little avail in many of the calamities to which mankind are liable; yet riches are able to solder up abundance of flaws. "Look you, friend Sancho," said the duke, "I can give away no part of heaven, not even a nail's breadth; for God has reserved to himself the disposal of such favors; but what it is in my power to give, I give you with all my heart; and the island I now present to you is ready made, round and sound, well proportioned, and above measure fruitful, and where, by good management, you may yourself, with the riches of the earth, purchase an inheritance in heaven."

"Well, then," answered Sancho, "let this island be forthcoming, and it shall go hard with me but I will be such a governor that, in spite of rogues, heaven will take me in. Nor is it out of covetousness that I forsake my humble cottage and aspire to greater things, but the desire I have to taste what it is to be a governor."

"If once you taste it, Sancho," quoth the duke, "you will lick your fingers after it; so sweet it is to command and be obeyed."

"Faith, sir, you are in the right," quoth Sancho; "it is pleasant to govern, though it be but a flock of sheep."

SPAIN, once mistress of the world, as were each in turn Chaldea and Carthage, Egypt, Greece, and Rome, has still remaining some of the great achievements of the human race. Many of these, it is true, were the work of Arabs, and the crowning glory of the nation came in the form of a gift from a Genoese sailor; nevertheless the Spanish monarchs had many shiploads of gold to spend, which it was hardly possible to do without leaving something whereby to remember them, though it were but a plat upon the perspective of history, like the huge Escurial, erected in honor of a saint. Yet for all that can be said, Spain's glory was very great; likewise her power and her wealth; for great and singular had been opportunity, of which to some extent she made avail. The harvesting, temporal and spiritual, begun by Ferdinand and Isabella at Granada, and continued by Charles V and Philip II, was the result of a long seed time and rare good fortune — seven centuries of what proved in the main successful warfare and half a world thrown like a gift into the lap of several sovereigns for him to accept who would.

Without able rulers, opportunity would have availed little; and Spain had able rulers, had great and gifted men for monarchs, though more who were insignificant and detestable; yet the foolish kings did not always bring on the nation her most grievous calamities, nor were the wisest always wise; better far had their catholic Majesties kept their Moors and Jews for useful labor, and let go the many golden isles and lands beyond the seas which finally wrought their country's undoing.

In the evolution of the modern Spaniard the old Iberian and Celt, or Celtiberian, united with the Carthaginian, Greek, Roman, Vandal, Goth, and Arabian, all of widely different races, contributed of their characteristics, the Romans in the main redominating. Thus to the Roman the

CHARLES V

Spaniard owes his stateliness and pride, to the Arab his fiery temperament and much of art and learning, while in his national institutions are traces of Teutonic influence.

Soil, climate, and whatever goes to make up the natural wealth of a country were better in Spain before her forests were destroyed, and dry and desolating winds permitted to sweep at random over sierra and plateau. Vast areas became valueless, or less valuable, as happened on the elevated table-lands of La Mancha and Castile, though still are fair forests of oak and other merchantable woods in the Sierra Nevada, the Sierra Morena, and the Pyrenees. The varied configuration of the Spanish peninsula, the varied origin of populations, and the conditions of settlement united to form widely different peoples. There are the lofty Pyrenees along the northern boundary, and in the south, rising from the heated plains of Andalusia, the chill summits of the Sierra Nevada; there are the central high plateau, the intersecting lesser sierras, the low well-watered plains, and the warm fertile valleys. Cut into physical divisions internally, the peninsula is likewise separated by physical barriers from the rest of the world. The five large and five lesser rivers are of little value as navigable streams; there are many salt lakes, especially in Catalonia and Aragon, and of mineral springs there are 2,000 or more.

Hence, as I have said, the varied Peoples and conditions, — the rugged Basque, prepared for the cold blasts from the Atlantic, and the sparkling Andalusian, his blood warmed by the sensuous breezes from the Mediterranean: the grave and thrifty Catalonian, the humble and hard working Galician, and the proud native of Aragon. Along the eastern or Mediterranean side, in an atmosphere pure and brilliant, grow olives and oranges, cotton and sugar-cane, date-palms and bananas; Valencia is an African garden set in a Sicilian landscape; here and at the northern end are golden grain, the vine, and all tropical fruits and nuts, — pomegranates and pineapples, figs, dates, almonds, and the like. Andalusia is a paradise of perennial youth and freshness, a paradise also of luxury and laziness.

On the western or Atlantic seaboard of the peninsula are raised in profusion grain, fruits, and the vine, with trees of hardy growth, as the oak and chestnut. There are still in Catalonia forests of beech and pine; Biscay is also well wooded; the two Castiles are almost bare of woods; Aragon produces grain, flax, hemp, the vine, and dye-stuffs, and affords pasture for sheep and cattle. Galicia on its limited area of arable land, raises fruits in abundance, as well as wheat, barley, corn, and flax. The Gallejos, as the inhabitants are called, are the servants of Spain, and speak a dialect different from others; the men swarming at certain seasons of the year into the towns of Spain and Portugal, where they find work, leaving their

FIG TREE

wives to conduct affairs at home. Estremadura, encircled by mountains, has a fertile soil which produces wheat and barley, but the people are improvident, and when inclined to industry in any form prefer the raising of sheep and cattle. Indeed the high plateaus are almost entirely given up to this industry, migratory flocks and herds roaming over the country to the injury of all who attempt legitimate farming. Murcia, Granada, and Valencia cultivate mulberry trees for silkworms. Leon, in the Pyrenees, where Pelayo lived and planned the future redemption of Spain, is unfitted for husbandry through extremes of heat and cold, in early times breeding only patriots. In Navarre grain, hemp, flax, wine, oil, and liquorice are produced. Murcia has little good land except on the banks of streams, but is well supplied with minerals.

Metals and minerals are well distributed in many portions of Spain, though at present but little worked; iron in Biscay, silver in Andalusia; gold, pearls, and rubies, copper, coal, and petroleum, cinnabar and marble at various points. The rich mines of gold and silver which attracted the ancients to these shores are, with the exception of the silver mine of Guadalcanal and the gold mine of Adissa in Portugal, either exhausted or abandoned; but the more useful metals are found throughout the peninsula, with precious stones in places. The best lead mines are at Linares and in the Sierra de Gador. Tin ores are worked on a small scale in Galicia; near Oporto is good coal; also in Aragon, La Mancha, and Asturias.

From the earliest times of which we have record the Carthaginians, and after them the Romans, knew of and worked the gold and silver mines of Spain, traces of their engineering achievements, still in existence, commanding our astonishment. In the Sierra Morena are rich deposits of gold, silver, iron, copper, and lead, and the quicksilver mines of Almaden gave to the Roman women the cinnabar with which they delighted to redden their hair, just as the savages of California resorted to the spot called by white men New Almaden for material wherewith to paint their faces.

At least a thousand years before the Christian era Phoenician navigators took possession of the Mediterranean seaboard, of Granada, Murcia, Valencia, and founded colonies, notably Tartessus, or Tarshish, and Gades, or Cadiz, where figured the Tyrian Hercules. The metalliferous Gaudalquiver attracted their attention, and Malaga, Cordova, and Seville show signs of Phoenician presence. A century later appeared the Greeks, and established themselves, among other places, at Emporiae that is to say Ampurias, on the coast of Catalonia, and Saguntum, later Murviedro, in Valencia. Then came the Carthaginians, led by Hamilcar and Hasdrubal, and and planted a new Carthage on the Spanish shore, teaching the rude tribes how to work their mines and grow grain, giving in exchange for their products goods from Tyre and old Carthage. Presently the Carthaginians dominated not only the natives, but the colonies of all other nations; for their city had become strong and rich, was well fortified, and commanded an extensive commerce. The Greeks appealed to Rome for protection, and the Punic wars followed, in which the Scipios finally gained possession of the coast from the Pyrenees to Cartagena, but not until after a death struggle with Hannibal, the Carthaginian. Not many years later Rome was in possession of the entire peninsula, except the Basque provinces, and during this conquest occurred many brilliant episodes, as the storming of Cartagena, the treasure city of the Punic provinces, and the vast riches secured by Publius Cornelius Scipio.

The Carthaginians vanquished and the country finally reduced to submission after many a vain attempt to shake off the yoke. Spain became one of the richest of Roman possessions, at once a source of supply and a seat of Roman learning, where were born Trajan and Hadrian, Quintilian and Martial, where Cato was consul, and over which Pompey and Caesar quarrelled. Among Greek and Roman remains, are those of Murviedro, or Old Walls, showing where 2,100 years ago stood Saguntum, a powerful and opulent city, strongly walled, and with aqueduct, amphitheatre, palaces, and temples. Also there is the palace of Augustus at Tarragona, now serving as a prison; the Trajan arch of Tiara; the bridges of Alcantara, Salamanca, and Calatrava; the aqueducts of Tarragona and Seville; the

CATO

bridge and aqueduct of Evora and of Segovia. On every side we have material evidence of the presence of the Goths; and as for the Arabs, take away their palaces and mosques, their

ROMAN AQUEDUCT, SEGOVIA

thousands of artistic treasures, and we lose much that is best worth preserving in the art and architecture of Spain.

Christianized in the time of Constantine, Spain has ever since remained intensely Christian. Upon the fall of Rome the German tribes found little difficulty in taking possession of the peninsula, the Suevi occupying Galicia, the Alani Portugal, and the Vandals Andalusia. The Romans appealed for aid to the Visigoths, or western Goths, then in the south of France, and soon these people were masters of the peninsula, Euric, the greatest of their kings, putting an end to Roman rule in 471, and giving a code of laws to Spain. Another famous Gothic king was Leovigild, who held court at Toledo, and was the first to array himself in royal purple and occupy a throne.

Among Gothic customs was the execution of such kings as did not please them, and to prevent his own assassination, Leovigild had a number of his nobles put out of the way from time to time, until he felt himself firmly seated in his chair of state, making Toledo his capital.

Standing, as did ancient Rome, on a circle of seven hills, and encompassed on three sides by the Tagus, spanned toward the east by a gigantic Moorish bridge in a single arch with the towers on its ancient ramparts half Gothic, half Arabic, with its forest of church pinnacles and the red walls of its Alcazar towering above city and river, Toledo presents a

most picturesque and imposing aspect. Enter, and you find yourself thrown back more than 2,000 years into the heart of the past. Captured by the Romans some two centuries before the Christian era, it became alternately the capital of Visigoth, Moorish, and Spanish kings, the impress left by each still visible, and

TOLEDO

the religio-military spirit of the stern and sombre middle age still conspicuous. As might be expected, there is in its by-ways and buildings an admixture of the royal and episcopal; palaces and churches mingling with fortress and convents; high, top-heavy houses with roofs projecting over secretive melancholy streets, with 20,000 sombre-visaged inhabitants where in the days of Mohammedan domination were 200,000 contented and prosperous people. On a mountain spur guarding the town is the ruined castle of Cervantes, and at its foot, closed at either end by a gate tower, the bridge of the bridge, as the Alcantara is sometimes called. At a bend of the terraced road is seen through the transparent atmosphere the Puerto del Sol, a massive Moorish gateway of rich orange red color embossed with finest tracery. All is of striking aspect as we proceed, the massive and gloomy buildings of mediaeval architecture, in the midst of which is the zocodover, or Moorish plaza, overhung in places by balconies, and whence the only wide street leads to the ever obtrusive cathedral with its crowd of filthy, whining beggars. Though to some extent stripped of its decorations, there is still much to admire in this cathedral, with its picturesque interior containing 100 columns, its sculptured figures, its spacious naves, carved stalls, and glass sparkling in ruby, sapphire, and emerald hues. Behind the Puerto del Sol is the church of El Christo de la Luz, once a mosque with low vaulted nave and graceful Moorish arches.

As the light of the Goths expires, the star of the East arises. Roderic, the last of the Gothic Kings, is betrayed by Count Julian, whose daughter he had seduced, to the Moors, already threatening the portals of the peninsula and in a battle of seven days duration, fought at Xeres de la Frontera in 711, the Gothic sovereign appearing in an ivory chariot drawn by milk-white mules at the head of 90,000 men, the fate of Spain is determined. Roderic is defeated; the Moors under Taric take possession of the country, and for the next seven centuries Spain is given over to Islamism. Christ the crucified is put away, and the watchword becomes "God is great and Mohammed is his prophet!" Art and architecture change with the mutation of religions; now the cathedral is a mosque only for the mosque in due time to become again a cathedral.

Xeres, that is to say Sherry; rather, the first speaking of the word Sherry was an abortive attempt to say Xeres — is today a very wealthy little town, the richest in Spain, if not in the world, for its size, and all by reason of its wines, of which the land thereabouts produces 2,000,000 gallons a year, the choicest vintages when ten of twelve years old selling for as much as $20 a gallon. After saying this, it is barely worth while to speak of the woollen stuffs and the morocco there manufactured, or of the grain there grown and exported. The wine interest is mainly in the hands of foreigners; and glory enough it is for one little town to make the good liquor which connoisseurs everywhere like so well to drink.

After gaining the victory over Roderic, Taric somewhat exceeded the authority given him by his master Musa, chief general of the Moslem forces in Africa, taking possession of Seville, Merida, and other cities; but was not severely censured for his transgression. Malaga offered no resistance; Granada was taken by storm; Cordova fell after feeble resistance, and in five years the entire peninsula, with the exception of Asturia, Cantabria, and Navarre, came under the new domination. At first the conquered country belonged to the caliphate of Bagdad; but in 756 an independent caliphate was established at Cordova by Abderrahman I, and under the third Abderrahman, and his son Hakem II, attained to great prosperity.

The old towns of Spain have each its several histories. In Roman Cordova, for example, were born Seneca and the poet Lucan; Arabian Cordova was the rival of Bagdad  and Damascus, the capital of the Ommiades, the birthplace of Avenzour and Averroes, the cradle of captains, the nurse of science, and for three centuries the home of wealth, learning, and refinement. Spanish Cordova, living largely on the glories of what had gone before, brought forth Juan de Mena, Ambrosio Morales, and the great captain, Gonzalez. It is today a city of the past, a city dead but not buried; grass grows in the streets, and

LUCAN

where were formerly 200,000 bright and active minds, 40,000 dull-witted citizens doze away their harmless lives. Of all its ancient glories there remains little of mark except the mosque, which in some respects is unrivalled. The building was founded, it is said, in 786 by the first Abderraman, who worked at it with his own hands for an hour every day and spent thereon 100,000 pieces of gold. It was

INTERIOR OF MOSQUE, CORDOVA

intended to rival the mosque at Bagdad in architectural and decorative scheme, and successive sultans contributed freely for its construction and support. La Mezquita, it is called, from the Arabic mezgad, to worship. The site was first occupied by a Roman temple of Janus; then by a cathedral, which became a mosque, afterward to be again transformed into a cathedral. The Arabs were more tolerant of the faith of their vanquished foes than the Christians later proved themselves to be. When in the eighth century the Moors took Cordova, and found there this cathedral, they deprived the Christians of only half their place of worship, leaving them to use the remainder as they chose. Later, wishing to make of it a beautiful temple, they paid them well for their portion, enough indeed wherewith to build a better church elsewhere.

Cordova has now some 50,000 inhabitants; when the Moors were in possession the population was 1,000,000, with hundreds of mosques, 28 suburbs, 113,000 houses, and 1,000 public baths. Among royal abodes were the palace of Contentment, the palace of Flowers, and the palace of Lovers; there were also a thousand mansions belonging to the rich and noble, some of them opening on the river on one side and with a garden on the other; not a few being connected with the sultan's mosque by vaulted passages, carpeted and lighted by jewelled lamps, while the ceilings of others rested on columns of marble or porphyry. It is said that on the palace which Abderrahman built for his best beloved, Zahra, 10,000 men and 4,000 horses labored for a quarter of a century. There were 15,000 bronze doors covered with silken portieres, and in the room called the caliph's hall was a lake of quicksilver of dazzling brilliance, Zahra's servants numbering 10,000 males and 6,000 females. The throne was resplendent with gold and gems; Persian rugs covered the mosaic floors, and around the main edifices were 1,000 pavilions and terraced gardens.

A native is rich with very little in Cordova; a few pesetas will buy him dried fish and oranges for a month, and the king can find no greater comfort than hundreds of beggars derive from sunning themselves in the alameda, or in the court of the mosque, where for 900 years has sparkled the fountain which waters the tall cypresses and palms. One may still lose oneself in the interior of this massive pile if care be not taken; of the forest of pillars, 1,200 in number, of jasper marble and porphyry, which originally separated the 40 or 50 transverse naves, 1,000 still remain. In the little Ceca chapel, under a shell-like roof carved from a single block of marble and adorned with mosaics sent by Romanus II from Constantinople, was kept the *Koran*; and near by, paved with silver, was the chapel of the Maksurah, where the caliph worshipped. There were many beautiful and holy things in this temple when the Moslems were there, one being a stand for the *Koran*, costing, it is said, a sum equal to $5,000,000, as money is counted at the present day.

The intelligent reader will doubtless form his own opinion as to the truth of these Arabian stories; but certain it is that at this period luxurious living reached an extreme point; for here were present all the conditions of luxury and excess, — money, power, beautiful women, passions with all the means at hand for their utmost gratification, art, science, and learning; in a word, material for the complete indulgence of every appetite, physical or intellectual.

Abderrahman I was a hard worker, and became a very rich man; indeed all Spain was his, or as much of it as he chose to take, the gold of Jew or Christian being equally at his disposal. He loved poetry as well as money, and gave himself to works of public utility, building dykes along the Guadalquiver, and planting in Spain the date-palm and other trees of oriental origin.

Hakem II, son and successor of Abderrahman III, who reigned at Cordova in true oriental state, was a learned man and a patron of literature, having agents at Damascus, Cairo, and Bagdad who bought or copied all the best works that could be found. A portion of his office was occupied as library and workshop, and filled with copyists, illuminators, and binders. His volumes numbered 400,000, and 44 others were filled with the catalogue. Schools were established; and the university of Cordova, where were taught Arabian jurisprudence, Islamism, and poetry, became famed throughout the east as well as in the west. For several centuries the peninsula prospered under Saracen domination. Art and science went hand in hand with commerce and agriculture, and so famous became the educational institutions of the Spanish Mohammedans that students flocked to their colleges from every quarter of Europe. In 1031, with the deposition of Hakem III, the decline of the caliphate began, the former provinces becoming independent kingdoms, of which there were twenty, those of Toledo, Saragossa, Granada, Seville, Cordova, and Valencia being among the number.

As the Greeks brought culture into Italy, so the Arabs brought learning into Spain. Besides law, theology, poetry, art, and architecture, the latter were well advanced in all the sciences. At Seville, in 1196, was erected by Geber the first astronomical observatory of which we have authentic record. Among other branches, his countrymen — though whether Geber was an Arabian is a matter of dispute — were skilled in mathematics, hydraulics, medicine, metallurgy, and chemistry. They constructed great systems of irrigation and were deft workers in gold, silver, copper, steel, and porcelain. At Cordova they tanned leather with pomegranate rind, and this was highly valued. But in nothing were the Arabs so expert as in architecture; for not satisfied with what they already knew when they set forth on their campaigns, the grand and beautiful buildings found in conquered cities incited them to build others yet grander and more beautiful, the means obtained from the subjugation of wealthy nations amply sufficing for the gratification of their tastes. Moreover, the foremost architects and artisans of the foremost nations, Grecian, Persian, Syrian, were ever at their command; hence the splendid specimens of Moslem art seen in the palaces and mosques of Mecca and Medina, Jerusalem and Damascus, Constantinople and Granada.

MALAGA

The country between Cordova and Malaga is fertile, producing in abundance; hence and for other reasons the latter is a great and prosperous city, its exports of wine and raisins being especially large. In the alameda is a fountain brought by Charles V from Genoa, and a Graeco-Roman cathedral, built in the sixteenth century, stands on the site of a mosque near the Moorish quarter, in which is also the castle of Gibralfaro. As in other opulent cities of southern Europe and the East, where the inhabitants are thriftless, lazy, and improvident, commerce and manufactures are mainly in the hands of foreigners, who become wealthy and build for themselves elegant homes in the most desirable quarters.

As it comes to us in the sober narrative of history it is difficult to believe the account given of the development of commerce and industries, and the gathering of riches by the Moslems during the earlier part of their occupation. A country which today has but a scant population of 17,000,000 at most, had in the time of Augustus 70,000,000, and under the Arabs 100,000,000. The state revenues of the latter were equivalent to $40,000,000; there were thousands of silk and cotton factories; indigo and cochineal were cultivated; gold was taken from the Darro, coral from the coast of Andalusia, and pearls from Tarragona. Agriculture and stockraising assumed greater proportions even than mining and manufactures. A thousand cities flourished all over the land, and the smaller towns no man could number. Twelve thousand men in costly array, glittering in steel and gold, constituted the caliph's body guard.

While the Moslems are thus fattening on the fertile fields of Spain, wrapped in the enervating luxury which always precedes a nation's downfall, a few patriots under Pelayo still retain their nationality in the fastnesses of the Pyrenees. Limited at first to Oviedo, their kingdom is enlarged by the conquest of Galicia, with portions of Leon and Castile by Alfonso the Catholic, who thus becomes king of Austrias. Other small kingdoms spring up

FERDINAND V

in the northern provinces, as those of Leon, Navarre, and Catalonia, and later, Castile, Aragon, and Portugal. These and others at times uniting to fight the Moors, though more often making war on each other, gradually force southward the Saracens, enlarge the Christian dominion, and wrest piece by piece their native land from infidel rule. After a great

ISABELLA

victory gained over the Almohades at Tolosa the united Christian powers under the leadership of Alfonso IX of Castile, only Cordova and Granada are left to the Moors. Finally by the union of Ferdinand of Aragon with Isabella of Castile all Christian Spain is united into one kingdom.

While Christian and Moslem were thus engaged in the long struggle which was to determine forever the fate of Islam in Europe, all over the land cities and provinces were subject, as elsewhere, to the ebb and flow of fortune. Though dating back to earliest times, Barcelona is in aspect and character a modern rather than an ancient city, one of the few really prosperous and progressive towns in Spain; and this not because it is the capital of a province, the see of a bishop, and the residence of a captain-general, nor because of its university, its colleges, hospitals, orphanages, and other charitable institutions; but on account of its factories, especially of its manufactories of cotton, wool, and silk, causing the place to rank for many centuries as the commercial and industrial centre of eastern Spain.

Exceedingly rich also in earlier days was Alcala de Henares, with its 38 churches, its university rivalling in reputation and learning that of Salamanca, and its 19 colleges, among them San Ildefonso, founded by Cardinal Ximenes, with patios in Doric, Ionic, and Berruguete styles, a half Gothic, half Moorish chapel. Here was printed, at a cost of 52,000 ducats, the polyglot *Bible* known as the *Complutensian*. Though numbered with the cities of the past, Alcala still lives as the birthplace of Cervantes, the day being the 9th of October 1547, this fact being well established, notwithstanding that the honor is claimed by eight other cities, Seville, Toledo, and Madrid among the number.

Then there is Burgos, the former capital of old Castile, the city of the Cid, the city of ancient legends, with a weird uncanny past and a mouldy present. Everywhere are pointed arches, gates of pilgrimage and pardon, antique doorways, statues and seraphs; but most remarkable of all is the cathedral with its clustered spires and pinnacles, built in the most florid of Gothic styles and more than three centuries in the building. Though with a population diminished from 80,000 to less than 30,000, it has still a considerable trade, with exports of linens and woollens fashioned in imitation of English goods.

High in the pines under Guadarrama, and resting on the slope of the sierra, is the real sitio of La Granja, upon which Philip V spent some millions of pesos, and where, let us hope, he passed some happy days — if monarchs are ever happy. A pretty picture is this airy palace, a veritable chateau en Espagne, with its cluster of roof-points, its balconies and fountains, its classic Corinthian columns, and a garden sportive with graces and goddesses in marble and bronze.

Avila has streets of quaint old houses, little changed since Saracenic times, some of them handsomely ornamented, but for the most part plain, though occupied by wealthy families. There is a Gothic cathedral erected early in the twelfth century, and there are the usual churches with the usual apses and arches, lofty pinnacles, and stained-glass windows in doubtful taste. Still is preserved the ancient wall, with towers and breastwork, though much of the town is built outside its circuit. Beyond is a desert, or little more than a desert, affording scant means of support for the present population of 7,000 or 8,000 souls.

CLOISTERS, TARRAGONA

In the midst of Catalonian olive orchards stands Lerida, a picturesque pile of purple rock, 300 feet high, crowned by fortifications of heavy masonry, by a cathedral with lofty spire and cloistered arches, and at the base a line of antiquated houses, a quay, an old mill, and a yellow stone bridge, — a somewhat desolate, but to the artist a quaint and pleasing picture.

Tarragona has a fine cathedral, built in the years between 1089 to 1131, with rose windows and romanesque arches; there are also the chapel of Santa Tecla and the cloister, which with its arcaded court and garden is most attractive of all. On the shore of the sea, three miles away, is, as tradition relates, the tomb of the Scipios, a massive Roman structure like some of which traces are still to be found on the Appian way. There are hereabout the remains of many Roman monuments, buildings, bridges, and aqueducts, among others fragments of the palace which Augustus occupied a few years before the birth of Christ.

Among the mountains near Tarragona, on a lonely spot, where, as was said, mystic lights revealed the resting place of a pious hermit who there had taken refuge from the Moors, was founded in 1149 by Ramon Berenger IV, king of Aragon, what became in time one of the largest religious establishments in the world. Poblet was the hermit's name, and the place became known as the convent of Poblet. It was situated in a solitary dell amid tangled woods overhanging craggy hills, between which and the buildings were orange groves whose gnarled and venerable trees were twisted into fantastic forms. Succeeding monarchs each added something to the extent and magnificence of the buildings, or to the wealth and beauty of the place. It became to them not merely a royal retreat for penitential meditation and prayer, where for a time conventual life might be enjoyed with profit to the soul, but presently arose royal tombs on either side of the choir, and around the principal cloister dukes and grandees occupied each his chosen niche. Marquises and counts had burial ground assigned them around the apse; the place for famous warriors was in the nave and anti-chapel; a portion of the transept was dedicated to the bishops of Lerida and Tarragona; while the abbots of Poblet, mightier and more honored than archbishop, prince, or potentate, reserved for themselves the chapter-house, their imposing effigies significant of strength and dignity. But in this Westminster abbey thus planted among the mountains of Spain, shrine or cemetery was not all nor the greater part of Poblet. It was a place of happiness for the living, as well as of rest for the dead. Its fame was noised abroad, and its wealth and magnificence increased, until among the regular occupants were numbered 500 monks of St. Bernard, who arrayed themselves in costliest robes and fed on the fat of the land. Far and wide extended the conventual domains, and the vestures and church furnishings were the richest that money would purchase. Books were gathered, until the Poblet library became one of the best in Spain. Vineyards were planted on the mountain sides, presses were erected, and great cellars were filled with the vintage which under the name of Priorato was most in favor of all the choice wines of the peninsula.

More and more reserved and exclusive became these monks of Poblet. The number was reduced from 500 to 66, and none were admitted to the fraternity save those of noble blood. Each had two servants, and all rode on milk-white mules, the latter being in the eyes of the vulgar almost as sacred as their riders; for such animals commanded enormous prices, and Spain was ransacked to secure them. Traffic and the useful arts were the handmaids of religion, and the holy men were served by those who ministered to their needs. Hospitals and houses of entertainment were erected for the use of pilgrims; likewise a palace for sovereigns, grandees, and men of royal lineage; for these also had bodies to feed and souls to save in common with the poor and sick and suffering.

Thus were made gorgeous the appendages of righteousness, as immorality and crime came on apace under cover of still more stringent rules, sombre sanctimoniousness and external formalities being but a cloak for the raging fires of passion within. Sovereigns of sovereigns, dictators to monarchs and princes, the holy men of Poblet became yet more autocratic, as the wealth, power, and popularity of their convent increased, issuing their commands to rich and poor alike as from God's vicegerents on earth. And all the while their rules were apparently of the strictest; for herein lay one element of their strength and influence, the restrictions and penances laid upon themselves being likewise imposed upon others; so that the dictatorial spirit grew upon these pious power-loving mortals, even

DON CARLOS

politics and governments being largely influenced by them. Then darker and yet more sinister became their purposes and deeds, until presently it was noticed that some who entered the convent were never known to leave it. Where were they and what were these fearsome mysteries about which men were whispering? The wars of Don Carlos brought on the climax; among the monks of Poblet dissensions and divisions arose; some were Carlists, some for the opposition, and all were ready for the agencies of knives, dungeons, and tortures. Things went from bad to worse until the country around became thoroughly aroused, and men of authority and power were filled with horrible suspicions.

And so one night there came to the convent a roaring multitude of country people, townsfolk, and men at arms, and breaking down the doors they poured through court and cloisters into the rack-rooms and dungeons, where they found human bones and emaciated forms, with such dreadful enginery of torture and cruelty as set them wild with fury. "To the ground with the accursed pile!" they cried, and straightway the work of demolition began, and ceased not until proud Poblet, with all its wealth of luxury and beauty strewed the convent grounds. Books were brought out and burned; shrines and statues, pictures, altarpieces, and priceless works of art and ornament fell under the general demolition, the destruction being finished by setting fire to the buildings, and burning all that could be consumed.

What now remains? The very abomination of desolation, says Augustus Hare. The old olive trees still line the rugged rock-hewn way of approach, and beyond projecting buttresses are the hills glowing in perennial verdure. Tall crosses rise on lofty pedestals, stained with golden lichen, myrtle, and lentisck, while at the cross-ways are groups of saintly figures amid the solitary groves where friars loved to walk. An avenue with broken seats at intervals on either side leads up to the convent walls, a clear sparkling mountain torrent surging by its side, overflowing a basin filled with ferns and fall water plants. After skirting the enclosure for some distance, the visitor is admitted by an ancient gateway to the ruins of the interior where the story of the past is written on rifted walls filled with fragments of sculpture of rare beauty and delicacy, on the ruins of spacious courts, of

SARAGOSSA

numberless cloisters, of broken marble pillars and stone-work with exquisite tracery everywhere strewing the ground. Still may be seen the little decorated chapel of St. George; the remains of frescoes telling of the Moorish invasion; towers, broken statues, and the bare skeleton of the hospital, while around the tombs of kings donkeys have now their stalls.

One can see much of Spain in Saragossa. Though modernized in places there are still marks of mediaeval

Christianity intermingled with traces of Moslem supremacy, relics of the auto-da-fé and inquisition standing forth in unpleasant contrast with the milder memorials of the followers of the prophet. Crossing the bridge from the grand plaza, there is on the left the cathedral of El Seo, which with the archiepiscopal palace and the lonja, or exchange, occupy conspicuous places in the square. Entering from the yellow sunlight the sombre vaults of the cathedral, visions of beauty and grandeur float before the eye as though descending from another sphere. Under Gothic arches and among shrines and altars are renaissance sculptures with bas-reliefs and paintings by the great masters. More celebrated even than the Seo is Nuestra Dama del Pilar, with its Byzantine suggestions, yellow varnished tiles, and domes resplendent in orange, green, and blue. The shrine, to which thousands of pilgrims resort, is of itself a temple within a temple, where the virgin appears descending on a pillar, arrayed in velvet and brocade and resplendent in gold and diamonds. The streets, market-places, statues, and towers are unique, and life in this old Aragonese town is seen as only it can be seen in Spain. In the suburbs is Aljaferia, the ancient palace of the kings of Aragon, now used as a barrack, the kitchen having been once a Moorish pavilion with beautiful arabesques, and the boot-room the chamber where Isabella, queen of Portugal, was born. The palace and prison of the inquisition were likewise a part of this now dishonored pile, whence thousands of human souls have been sent with cries of agony into the unknown.

In the old Castilian town of Segovia, with its cathedral of many pinnacles and its ancient amphitheatre, a Trajan aqueduct of gray and black granite blocks cemented together and with arches a hundred feet high attest the solidity of Roman workmanship. Near the convent of San Gabriel this aqueduct serves as a bridge, underlying which are 320 arches, in double rows, one superimposed upon the other, some of them having been destroyed when the Saracens plundered Segovia. In 1483 Isabella ordered them to be restored; but even now the Roman arches can readily be distinguished from the Spanish, owing to the inferiority of the latter. It is a crowded town, red roofed houses jostling each other, and all intermingled with old romanesque churches and high lofty towers. In 1494 the marquis de Villena built at the end of the alameda the Geronimite monastery of El Parral, in token of gratitude to heaven for enabling him to overcome three antagonists at once in a duel fought upon its site. It is regarded as one of the most remarkable buildings in Spain; and though parts of it have disappeared through vandalism and decay, there still remain the carved pulpit of the refectory, the cloisters, and a room fitted up as a pantheon, filled with monuments of legendary and local lore. In 1204 was erected by Honorius II the Vera Cruz,

ALCAZAR, SEGOVIA

copied after the church of the holy sepulchre in Jerusalem. Not far from the site of the old alcazar, whence Isabella went forth to be proclaimed queen of Castile, are the tower of San

Esteban and the cathedral, begun in 1525, and one of the last of the great Gothic structures of Spain. As with many other cities, Segovia under Saracenic rule was rich and prosperous; at one time 25,000 pieces of cloth were made there annually, giving employment to 14,000 workmen; now not more than 200 pieces are manufactured, and the place is but a shadow of its former self.

In the fourteenth century the university of Salamanca had 10,000 students; now it has 1,000; the collegiate buildings were palaces of learning; now they are for the most part in ruins, or let to poor families, though one is occupied by a governor and another as a college. And the decay continues; opposite the university buildings, or what is left of them, is the cathedral, gorgeous in yellow stone and florid Gothic detail. The plaza of Salamanca, among the largest in Europe, is surrounded with Corinthian arches, the municipal buildings occupying one of the sides. There are two cathedrals, of which the older structure belongs to the thirteenth century and is a fine specimen of the later romanesque. Worthy of mention also is the bridge across the Tormes, 500 feet long and with arches of Roman workmanship, for this is one of the oldest of Spanish towns.

The church of Santa Catalina, at Valencia, which stands on the site of a Roman temple of Diana, is thrown into the shade by its octagonal Gothic tower, called El Miguelete from the first ringing of its bells on San Miguel's day. It was intended to be carried up 350 feet, but reached a height of only 160 feet. For forty miles around Valencia the country is a garden of orange groves and vineyards, the irrigating canals constructed by the Moors retaining the fertility of a soil naturally rich. Water is a fundamental source of wealth throughout the larger part of the peninsula, and such is the quantity diverted from the streams for agricultural purposes that when the rivers reach the sea their volume is greatly diminished. Its use is regulated by law, the water-court of Valencia, composed of twelve farmers, meeting once a week to settle disputes. The houses of the old nobility have Gothic windows and open arcades in the upper story, a style of architecture that finds no favor with the modern Spaniard.

French invasion and the vis inertiae, nowhere more palpable than in Spain, have reduced to a wreck the capital of Juan II of Castile, glorious in the days of Charles V and Philip II. Yet the broad plaza of Valladolid is pleasant to look upon, and still there remains Herrera's imposing cathedral founded in 1585. More beautiful is the church of Santa Maria de la Antigua standing near it. Then there is the Dominican convent of San Pablo, rebuilt in 1463 by Torquemada, patron of art and promoter of autos-da-fé for the spiritual

SEVILLE

60

delectation of his patroness Isabella the Catholic. The city can boast of the university and royal palaces which once were there, while pointing to the tiered balconies, shops, and arcades, the theatres, libraries, and picturesque plazas which abound in the modern city.

With the consolidation of petty provinces and kingdoms, and the union of Aragon and Castile, a new nation comes upon the scene. Already former sovereigns of Castile had wrested from the Moors Cordova, Seville, Cadiz, and other Saracenic possessions in southern Spain, and had attached them to their dominions. When Seville was taken by the Castilians, it was in truth a beautiful city, much larger than at the present day, and inclosed within a Moorish wall having sixty-six towers and fifteen gates, while the city itself was teeming with life and gaiety, and beyond was the broad valley of the Guadalquiver, verdant with olive and orange orchards, palm-groves and vineyards. Sephela, the Carthaginians called it, erecting to Astarte, goddess of love, a temple which has since done service as a Roman fane, a Gothic church, a Moorish mosque, and now a catholic cathedral, with a tower 350 feet in height, two large organs, and a library. A noted spot is that where the Carthaginians used to burn their children to please their god, afterward used as a parade ground for Roman soldiers, as a barrack for Moorish cavalry, and later as a bull-ring capable of seating 11,000 persons. A tall structure is the so-called Tower of Gold, built by the Romans and used as a place of observation, whence looking down on the paradise that lay below, the observer was fanned by fresh, cool breezes, from the silvery Guadalquiver winding through fragrant gardens of fruits and flowers.

At Seville one sees at his best the gay and volatile Andalusian, with his mercurial temperament and happy environment, a type as different from the old Castilian as Segovia is different from Seville; quite different both from those who dwell in the sombre shades of Cordova and Granada. Probably no city in Europe was more greatly affected by New World influence than Seville, and the effects of that influence are seen today in the crowded streets, the busy shops, and general air of alertness among the people, so greatly in contrast with the general apathy of the orthodox Spaniard.

Seated by the Guadalquiver, smiling in the sunshine, the very name of Seville is significant of all that is bright and beautiful. The place is as full of happy life as is Burgos of mournful meditation. White houses with green balconies embellished with flowers and filigree line the clean shaded streets, while the patios and plazas with their cooling fountains are perfumed by the orange or citron, the banana and almond trees, through whose foliage flit birds of sweet song and bright plumage.

ALCAZAR

Though there is so much in Seville that is American there is more that is Arabian, many of the people being proud of their Saracen antecedents. The streets and shops are Moorish, and care is taken to preserve Moorish edifices in all their characteristic originality; pride being taken even in the construction of the narrow streets which render this "oven of Spain" not only endurable but to the native comfortable during the hot months of summer. Next to the Alhambra of Granada, the Alcazar of Seville is the finest monument of Arabian architecture. After suffering disgraceful devastation and abuse, the edifice has of late years been restored by the duke of Montpensier, so that it is now like a palace of the fairies, its walls seemingly covered with silk and gold. The pavement of the patio is of marble, having in the centre a fountain surrounded with beds of flowers, the gallery resting on graceful columns supporting open arcades. This Alcazar, Al Kasr, or house of Caesar, though begun in 1181, was in great part rebuilt under the direction of Moorish architects by Pedro the Cruel, a tyrant full worthy of his cognomen.

As with the Alcazar, so with the Giralda tower, said to surpass in beauty and harmony all Christian belfries. So lofty is it that the detail of Arabic ornament on pale pink is soon lost to the eye, and so spacious that one may ride on horseback to the summit. From the top may be seen the whole city, and the graceful Guadalquiver winding among the fruitful plantation bordered with aloes. There are ninety-three stained windows in the cathedral, and every chapel is a gallery of painting and sculpture. In architecture it is of the simplest Gothic, though built upon the site of the ancient mosque, as before stated, and preserving its walls and porticos and Moorish arch. The tower is used as the campanile of the cathedral. Built by the caliph Yakub-al-Mansour about the year 1200, it is square in

ALCAZAR GARDENS, SEVILLE

form and was intended for an observatory. The services in the church are equalled only by those of St. Peter, the gigantic pipes of the two organs having been compared to the columns of Fingal's cave. The bronze image which surmounts the tower stands upon a dizzy height, the cathedral and tower being about equal to St. Paul's, but showing to better advantage on account of the large open space around them. The entire structure, which is 378 feet long and 254 feet wide, has been compared to a stately ship at sea under full sail. Nine doors lead into the court of Oranges, and within the church are five aisles in a maze of columns. In the choir are 117 carved stalls; in one of the chapels is a silver tabernacle, and in that which is known as the royal chapel are emblems and relics in gold and bronze. From the expenditure in past times at this sanctuary some idea may be formed not only of the piety but of the wealth of the worshippers. In the illumination 20,000 pounds of wax were annually consumed; 500 masses a day were said at 80 altars; and in the sacraments 18,000 litres of wine were used. The canons arrived in splendid equipages, and jewelled fans in the hands of smooth-visaged clerks cooled their brows during service. In the sacristy were priceless Murillos, rich vestments, and relics in gold and precious stones in profusion, a single article having 1,200 diamonds, while before one of the monuments, on certain occasions, 114 lamps and 453 tapers were burned. The tower, lifting its pinnacle in gray and yellow, has been likened to a spike of gold, its sparkle visible in the sunshine for miles around.

Two bridges cross the Guadalquiver at Seville, connecting the city with its gypsy suburb. In a stately building facing the botanical garden, one that might be taken for a royal

palace, is the government tobacco factory, where 6,000 women find work. Bronze, brass, pottery, glass, silk, and other articles are also manufactured. The palace of San Elmo, once an ancient college, is the residence of the duke of Montpensier, who has converted it to some extent into a museum, and surrounded it with park and garden of exquisite beauty. Not far away, and once a bastion of the Alcazar, is the Torre del Oro, before mentioned, so-called from the gilt tiles which roofed it, one says; but the name

INTERIOR, PALACE SAN ELMO, SEVILLE

is generally accredited to the storage here of precious metal as it came from the New World — gold principally, as there was also the tower of silver. The suburb of Triana was formerly defended by a castle where were first the headquarters of the inquisition at Seville.

PILATE'S HOUSE

To Seville Spain is indebted for many of her most illustrious painters and poets, among the former being Murillo, Velasquez, Zarbaran, and Cespedes, and among the latter Herrera, La Cueva, and Carvajal. Here also were born or lived men famous on sea and land, sailors and scientists, archbishops and generals, authors and adventurers. To Seville came Julius Caesar in 45 B.C., capturing and making of it a Roman colony as a foil to Cordova the favorite city of Pompey. The Goths at first established here their seat of government, afterward removing it to Toledo. It was held by the Saracens until 1248, when it fell into the possession of Ferdinand III of Castile. In 1810 it was plundered by the French under Soult, and despoiled to the value of $30,000,000. There are many monuments and buildings within its precincts worthy of mention — instance the hospital, founded by Miguel de Manana; the convent with its rare paintings; the Casa del Ajuntamiento, where the autos da fé took place, outside the walls. Then there is the casa de Pilato, or house of Pilate, built by the marquis of Tarifa in imitation of the so-called Pilate's house which he saw in Jerusalem in 1520, and later passing into the hands of the dukes of Medina Cali. In Seville lived, in 1196, a Moorish architect, Abu Jusuf Yacub, who built the Giralda tower and the great mosque, repaired the city walls and the Roman aqueduct, and constructed a bridge of boats across the Guadalquiver. The Alcazar was in part a Roman and in part a Moorish structure, with attempted restoration of the whole by the Spaniards.

Cadiz, founded by the Phoenicians, known as Gades to the Romans, when Spain became a Roman province conquered by the Arabs, and regained by the Spaniards in 1262,

CADIZ

came into prominence as the seaport of Seville during the palmy days of New World commerce. While still the chief commercial city of Spain, it was then the chief commercial city of the world. The entrance to the harbor from Puerto de Santa Maria is protected on either side by the forts of Matagorda and Puntales, among other points of interest being the navy yard and arsenal of La Caraca. As seen from the bay, with its spires and observation towers, it is in truth a beautiful city, though formed for utility, with great warehouses and factories for the making of fans, mantillas, gloves, and guitars. Hither for three centuries came the great galleons from Mexico and other parts of Spain's vast possessions, bringing gold to the value of thousands of millions of dollars.

The promontory of Gibraltar, which with Centa opposite was called by the ancients the pillars of Hercules, and supposed to be the western limit of the world, is a fortified rock 1,600 feet high and seven miles in circumference, occupied as a point d'appui by the English, and therefore, though properly a part of Spain, there is little that is Spanish about it. The rock is perforated with caverns; one side is almost perpendicular, while the other slopes to the water's edge, where are the town and principal fortifications. At the cost of immense sums of money, amounting, a score of years ago, to more than $250,000,000, the fortress has been made impregnable, galleries and passages being cut through it miles in extent and port-holes pierced for guns. While the Saracens were in possession they built a tower which still remains as the only surviving monument of the Moorish occupation.

GIBRALTAR

An ancient Arab writer says of Almeria, "It is a city where if thou walkest the stones are pearls, the dust gold, and the gardens a paradise." That is to say, apart from the oranges and figs and lemons which grew in abundance, it was an exceedingly prosperous place, made so largely no doubt by its being at that time a noted pirates' nest.

When we consider that the centuries of continuous warfare in Spain were largely for religion's sake, we are not surprised to find the priesthood occupying positions of authority and often amassing enormous wealth. The power wielded by Torquemada and Ximenes, which was something more than royal, inasmuch as it was superior to the mandates of earthly princes and potentates, are examples of what the clergy were able to accomplish during these times. To their credit, be it said, their means and influence were used in the main for worthy purposes, as for the support of hospitals and education, and to them is largely due the existence of many monuments of learning and charity.

Castile and the kingdoms adjacent had, besides the religious fraternities, a large class of the ricos hombres or higher nobility, including princes, who were exempt from fines, imprisonment, and taxation, and were little inferior to the king, often indeed disputing authority with him. There were likewise the inferior gentry, hidalgos and caballeros, who were of little use except as fighting men. All these the common people labored for and supported as their superiors; there was no strong, intelligent middle class, furnishing the wealth and controlling the policy of the government. But so it was everywhere in those days; and hence we see few great works among the earlier nations of the earth save temples, palaces, and tombs, little in the way of general utility or for the benefit of the people.

Chivalry arose, uniting the temporal and spiritual; the power of such institutions as the Hermanadad, and the military orders of Santiago, Calatrava, and Alcantara, with the wealth which they acquired, or might acquire, being limited only by the limit of their influence and prowess. Bringing into the field thousands of mailed knights, uniting to conquer and dividing to fight for the spoils, whatever they might win was theirs by right of conquest, and their castles, towns, and convents were numbered by thousands.

It now remained for Ferdinand and Isabella to bring to an end these seven centuries of war by attacking the Moslems in their last stronghold. Driven from every other part of Spain, the Moors had taken refuge in Granada, and unable there to maintain war against the Castilians, had sent them 12,000 ducats as annual tribute. The place was strongly fortified. There were 70,000 houses, enclosed by a high wall fifteen feet thick and three leagues in circumference, with 1,030 towers and twelve gates, and a fortified palace for a garrison of 40,000 men. In city and country were luxurious living and boundless prodigality. Even the lower class of women had anklets of silver and gold, while those of the upper class wore a profusion of jewelry, including finely wrought bracelets and girdles of gold studded with precious gems, with braided and bejewelled hair, and garments delicately fashioned of woolen and silk. The men were likewise brilliantly arrayed in clothes of finest finish, their scimitars and armour chased and enamelled, their daggers and sword-blades of Damascus steel, and their horses richly caparisoned.

It is on the purple-clad slope of the Sierra Nevada, about 2,500 feet above the sea, that this city stands; a city in whose history is much romance and in whose study is much of pleasure and profit. Well built houses of antique oriental construction line the narrow, crooked streets which lead from the principal plazas. After the Alhambra, of which I will presently speak further, the Moorish monuments in Granada are the old Saracenic post-office, the casa del Carbon, now a coal depot but once a beautiful structure with handsome Moorish gate; and the ancient silk market, with its columns and arcades producing a charming effect. Conspicuous among the buildings are Nuestra Senora de las Augustias, with its stately towers and richly decorated altar; the Gothic cathedral, embellished with jasper and colored marble, and the monastery of San Geronimo.

As early as the year 767 a castle was built there by Ibu-Abderrhaman, and in 1238 Ibrahim Ben Akmar, under the title of Mohammed I, founded the kingdom of Granada, which endured for two and a half centuries, or until the expulsion of the Moors by the catholic sovereigns. Within the lines marked out by the founder, this latter prince began the erection of the Alhambra, Kasr-al-hamra, or the Red Castle, so-called presumably from the red earth of which the bricks were made. The work was continued by succeeding rulers until 1333, when it was completed by Yusuf I; and then it was that Granada reached the height of her power and prosperity. Upon the fall of Cordova and Seville, 200,000 families took refuge there, and to these are probably due in part that internal dissension which rendered possible the conquest of Granada.

Few of the world's great monuments have held the interest and admiration of mankind so long and completely as the Alhambra. Elevated above the sultry plain, shaded by noble groves of elm, built in the most sumptuous of oriental designs and yet in exquisite taste, embowered in fragrant gardens made musical by the song of nightingales and the murmur of fountains, it would seem that if only walls could keep out wars and luxury could bring

KING CHARLES' PALACE, ALHAMBRA

content, here indeed was a glimpse of paradise such as should satisfy Mohammedan or Christian. On every side broad avenues cross each other and climb the wooded slopes, while stretches of lawn and bubbling brooks impart a freshness and fragrance to the air. The buildings, as they stand to-day, consist of four distinct palaces, three of them the old Moorish structures, and one, begun but never finished, belonging to the days of Charles V. Among the many towers were the Vermilion towers, the tower of the Infanta, the tower of the Vigil, of the Beaks, and of the Seven Portals, through which Boabdil, last of the Saracen rulers in Spain, took his departure as the Spanish army entered.

Approaching the Alhambra under a canopy of elms, along one of the several terraces on which the structure rests, entrance is made by the gate of Justice, or Babu shariah, the gate of the Law, as the Arabs called it, because, like the Jewish sovereigns, Moorish monarchs here settled disputes arising among their people. It was built in 148 by Abu el walid Yusuf, who wrote over the inner arch, "May the All-powerful make this gate a bulwark of protection, and record its erection among the imperishable actions of the just."

By a narrow vaulted passage is reached the upper esplanade, or place of Cisterns, with yellow towers enclosing the citadel on the left, and on the right the bright yellow stone structure of the Spanish monarch, the interior a circular court, the exterior a quadrangle, and beyond gardens and trees, a church convent and mosque, and a miniature town, all within the tower-girdled precincts of the castellated hill. In the court of myrtles, paved in blue and white, and in the centre of which is a pool with gold-fish, are some of the most exquisite specimens of Arabian art, their charms intensified by the luminous air. The largest patio is the court of Ambassadors, conspicuous for its arches and decorations. It is about 40 feet square, and the vaulted ceiling, of cedar incrusted with mother-of-pearl, is 75 feet high, filling the base of the tower of Comares, 200 feet in height, beneath whose shadow runs the Darro, roaring down the sierra with the fury of a mountain torrent. But most exquisite of all, and a masterpiece of Moorish art, is the court of Lions, surrounded by a portico with 124 columns, a marvel of elegance and beauty. Open arcades of graceful mould and airy lightness are supported by two pavilions projecting into the patio. Opening upon this court are several chambers of medium size — the hall of Two Sisters, the hall of the Abencerrages, the private apartments of the sultan; also the baths of the sultanas and the pavilion of the queen. The delicacy of finish in this part of the palace is exceeded only by the profusion of its decorations. Embroideries with interlacing designs emerging one out of another without beginning or end, in every pattern and color, cover walls, arches, gates, windows, and friezes.

The Alhambra is an oriental dream, a vision of eastern art and architecture nestling in this elevated foothill of the snowy sierra. The sunlight is rendered opaque and tremulous, the massive walls and narrow windows subduing the heat and light, which nevertheless make luminous the fountains. It is characteristic of eastern architecture to invent contrivances for keeping out the fierce rays of the sun, while providing space for cooling waters and fragrant flowers. In the ruins of Theban palaces the private apartments of sovereigns may be discovered by their narrow limits, low ceilings, and narrow windows; but Thebes was outdone by Granada in the blending of symmetry, grandeur, and wealth of decoration, united with comfort and luxury.

The principal Moorish street of Granada is El Zacatin, and near it are two narrow passage-ways, embellished in sculpture and stucco work and called El Alcaiceria, or the silk bazaar. The first archbishop of Granada was Isabella's confessor, Talavera, by whom was built in 1497 the church of San Geronimo for the purpose of converting the Moors. The Generalife, or architect's garden, as the word implies, was so-called by its original owner, an inspector of public works. It was afterward purchased and turned into a pleasure house by one of the Moorish monarchs. On the further side of the Darro are the quarters of the gypsies, whose houses are excavations in the rocks on the southern side of the hill of Albaicin.

Muley Abul Hassan ruled in Granada when in 1476 Ferdinand sent Juan de Vera to demand the annual tribute which had not been remitted of late. The kingdom then consisted of fourteen cities and several hundred fortified castles, so that Abul Hassan felt himself strong enough to defy the sovereign of Castile. Thus when Juan de Vera brought back the message of the ruler of the Moors, "Tell your master that they who pay tribute are dead; the mints of Granada now coin only swords," Ferdinand replied, "I will pick the seeds from this pomegranate one by one," Granada signifying the pomegranate, and the seeds the fortified castles.

This having been done, Muley Abul Hassan and Malaga being among the picked pomegranate seeds, in 1492 Ferdinand and Isabella appeared with their army before the walls of Granada to receive the keys of the citadel from Boabdil el Chiquito. The terms of capitulation were that Christian captives should be liberated, and the Moors become the subjects of Castile, to be governed by their own cadis, protected as to their prosperity and religion, and exempt from tribute for three years, after which they should pay only the same as to their former rulers, whosoever might desire to depart receiving free passage to Africa.

At the portal of the Seven Floors, as he came forth amid thundering of cannon into the presence of a vast multitude where mounted on richly caparisoned steeds were Ferdinand and Isabella, Boabdil said, as he presented the keys, "Thus ends the Arabian empire in Spain; God is great! Remember, O king, your promises." How the Spanish sovereigns kept their pledges history relates. Christian writers have stamped the Moor as cowardly, and so perhaps he was; but rather should we call him sick at heart on leaving home and country; for had not this beautiful land been his and his people's for nearly eight hundred years, a longer period than the Spanish nation had existed prior to the coming of the Moors? On leaving the palace forever, while turning to look upon it for the last time, he exclaimed, as the tears sprang to his eyes, "Allah; alas! it is the will of Allah; when was misfortune like mine?" Replied the mother, made of sterner stuff, "You do well, indeed, to weep like a woman for what you could not defend like a man!"

Two important events occurred while the Spanish sovereigns were at Granada; one was an edict expelling the Jews, and the other the agreement with Columbus concerning his voyage westward. The Jews were rich; Ferdinand and Isabella needed money, and it is never difficult to bring false charges or to reconcile the conscience to any wrong committed in the name of right. It was said that the Jews kidnapped Christian children; Isabella did not believe it when 30,000 ducats were offered by the Jews for permission to remain. She did not believe it even when her confessor Torquemada rushed into the presence of the sovereigns, saying, "Judas sold his master for thirty pieces; you would sell him for thirty thousand.'" Nevertheless she signed the decree for their expulsion, as did also her husband. A yet more serious charge against the two sovereigns was the breaking of their pledge to

the Moors, at the instigation of Ximines. After all the promises made, they were coolly informed that they must become Christians or leave the country; whereupon 3,000,000 took their departure, as the record stands, between 1492 and 1610. Neither Jew nor Moor were permitted to take with them their money or other valuables, and many thousands both of Moors and Jews were burned at the stake by order of Ferdinand and Isabella and their successors. Yet these unfortunates suffered for no crime; they were obedient, God fearing,

CARDINAL XIMENES

and hard working men, the best of farmers and artisans, and were more learned and refined than those who put them to death. Saving faith! which was the more efficacious, the faith of those who persecuted or of those who were persecuted for righteousness' sake?

After all that has appeared on the pages of history as to the abominations of the Arabs, their superstitions and polygamies, their Mecca pilgrimages and holy-sepulchre holding, much may be said in their favor. Compare Ibu-Abderrhaman's Alhambra with the Escurial of Philip II; the Cordova of Abderrhaman the Great with the Madrid of Charles V.

ESCURIAL

The Spanish kings, together with their people, fattened on the gold of America and fell into decay; the Moslems, it is true, had fattened and died before them, but their glory remains in visible form, in the libraries they founded, the schools they established, and the palaces and temples which they erected. But for their paving the way in promoting agriculture, commerce, and manufactures, and science, there would have been small achievements to record of the Spaniards who came after them. It likewise appears from the written pages even of European history that the plighted word, the charity and integrity of the Mohammedan were superior to those of the Christian. How wise and humane the policy of these followers of the prophet; how tolerant to the Spanish Christians, and also to the Jews, who were left to worship in their own way! No sooner had the Spaniards acquired the supremacy than their course was marked by fraud and treachery. Not only Moorish religion but Moorish civilization must be eradicated. Following the decree of 1492, aimed specially at the Jews, ordering all who did not become Christians to leave Spain in four months and forbidding them to carry away even their gold and silver, an edict which, according to the Spanish historian, Mariana, drove 50,000 families into exile, came the persecution of the

Arabs, who at the capitulation of Granada had been guaranteed all their civil rights, with freedom to worship, and non-interference with their customs. But with such monarchs as Ferdinand, and Isabella, and Philip, promises went for little. First the Moors were restricted in their worship; then in their language, their dress, and their amusements. It was part of the life of these sovereigns, of almost all sovereigns of that day and the days and years which followed, so to dictate and dominate as to make their people unhappy. The very fact that they lived honestly, labored faithfully, and were prosperous counted against them, And so the third Philip in 1609 drove out the Moors, huddled them on board and ship and cast them on desolate shores where many met their death. From the single province of Valencia went 140,000; Catalonia was well nigh depopulated; the Sierra Morena, covered with vineyards and cornfields, became a wilderness. To this day the curse of it remains; between Malaga and Granada, and all along the Guadalquiver where were thousands of villages and tens of thousands of happy homes there remain only a few wretched villages.

The successful expedition of Columbus was followed by the swarming of adventurers to the New World, who flooded Spain with the gold they

had gathered. The slave trade was also profitable, as was likewise the conversion of the Indians. Kings, clergy, grandees, and dukes became exceedingly rich. The higher nobility had large landed estates, many towns and villages, and large incomes. The half million dollars a year which the duke of Alva's income

DUKE OF ALVA   equalled, would buy as much as two millions at

GONSALVO
FERNANDEZ

the present day. Gonsalvo de Cordova's income, or rather that of his family, was almost as large, and that of the duke of Medina Sidonia was larger. The duke of Infantado could bring 30,000 of his own men into the field, while the archbishop of Toledo's revenue was equal to about $4,000,000 as now is the purchasing power of money. The Moors had lived extravagantly, but the Spaniards sought to outdo them. Rich clothing and the richest of fare, a profusion of costly jewels, and sumptuous dwellings with delicate carvings and mosaic floors, resulted from the conquests of Pizarro and Cortes.

With all their faults and follies, Ferdinand, Charles, and Philip were astute and powerful sovereigns, and under their rule Spain became very great. But a century of inactivity, luxury, and vice is more than any nation can endure without decay or death. It is the old story, with the inevitable result. Had Spain kept her Jews and Moors, kept in thriving condition her agriculture and manufactures, kept free her commerce, and been governed less by greed and fanaticism, she might have enjoyed a longer and a nobler supremacy. As it was, decadence began before the death of Philip, who indeed was somewhat decayed himself when death delivered the world of him. Under the third Philip, who was imbecile as well as fanatical, enjoying all his predecessor's vices with none of his virtues, the country lapsed into a state of absolute decrepitude. The absence of that healthful blood-letting which the Moors had so long administered, and the wars of Charles V with France, Germany, and the Netherlands, with Italy, Tunis, and Algiers had kept from too sudden stoppage, was one cause of disease. Then Philip III found 600,000 Moors who had been overlooked in the previous exterminations, and these he drove out, leaving the industries of Spain to the worthless remnant of the population. Philip IV lost Portugal; Germany and the Netherlands followed; then Naples and Sicily; then Sardinia, Parma, and Milan; then Gibraltar and Minorca, and finally most of India and America, — in all a quarter of the world, at least. But these losses of Spain can not be considered other than as a great gain to the world at large and the change came none too soon.

PHILIP IV

It is neither pleasurable nor profitable to follow the footsteps of a great nation in its decline. As notable specimens of folly, posterity points to the Escurial and the Arada. While Madrid was yet a hamlet, Burgos, Toledo, Seville, and Valladolid had been each in turn the Spanish capital. While Charles V was yet a boy, Cardinal Ximenes carried the government to Madrid, and later Philip II held court there, building his Escurial not far away, because, ill-natured people say, those were the most unpleasant places in Spain for the purpose. Spain has many interesting cities; but one of the least picturesque of all is Madrid, chosen as the capital because of the gout of Charles V. From the cowardice of Philip sprang the Escurial, and here we have the origin of these historic places.

Few subjects in history have been more severely criticised than Philip and his Escurial. Why should a monarch of limitless resources choose so desolate a spot for the site of a pleasure palace? asks one. Another calls it the architectural nightmare which Charles IV wisely declined to inhabit, building instead a pretty little toy palace of his own. Even the gardens with their box terraces show more of architecture than of flowers, while the books in the library are arranged with their backs turned to the wall. Doubtless Philip's greatest pleasure was in his heavenly meditations, for he was ever on serious thoughts intent, and as sombre minded as he was selfish.

If by his subjects esteemed as a great monarch, he was not, as I have intimated, a great warrior. While the battle of St. Quintin was raging, for instance, instead of joining in the fray, he found it more to his taste to remain at home and make vows to the virgin, — hence the origin of the Escurial, at once a royal palace and a monastery, for Philip in remembering his maker never forgot himself. It is an imposing pile, standing in grim solitude at the foot of the sierra de Guadarma, fourteen leagues west of Madrid, 3,683 feet above sea level, and was pronounced on its completion the eighth wonder of the world. Lorenzo — he who was roasted — was the saint to whom Philip believed himself specially indebted for victory; hence the stupendous mass of buildings with surpassing external decorations took the form of a gridiron, the interior being riddled with square courts. About a mile in circumference, the structure has 1,860 rooms, 12,000 doors and windows, 80 flights of stairs, 73 fountains, 48 wine cellars, 51 bells, 8 organs, and 1,560 oil and fresco paintings. There are also a library, a college, and the mausoleum of the Austrian and Bourbon kings of Spain. Into the wall near the top of one of the buildings the king had inserted a plaque of gold, three feet square and an inch in thickness, where age after age it glitters in the sun to the confusion of all who declared that this massive pile would be the builder's ruin. The convent, now deserted, was presented by Philip to the Hieronymites, one of the largest and richest of the religious orders in Spain, whose members, under the protection and regulation of St. Jerome and St. Augustine, devoted themselves to the advancement of science and agriculture.

In the midst of gardens and parks, not far from Madrid by rail, appear, like oases in the desert, the two palaces of Aranjuez, one a rambling chateau, the other the casa del Labrador, about a mile distant, made infamous by the doings of Charles III, Maria Louisa, and her lover Godoy. The low walls of the rooms are hung with elaborate silk embroidery, and in each of the smaller chambers are half a dozen clocks, several of the sovereigns of Spain having been possessed with a mania for time-pieces. Aranjuez has been called the Versailles of Madrid; but in truth it is as little like Versailles as Madrid is like Paris. The place is occupied only in the three months of summer, when the grass-grown streets lined by large low houses are alive with the gaiety of court and courtiers.

GODOY, GOYA

Under the reign of Charles II, the population of Spain fell in number to 8,000,000, and here is perhaps the most conclusive proof of what has been said, as to the wisdom and polity of the Arabs compared with the Spaniards. The Saracens found the peninsula in the half civilized half developed condition in which the wars and intermixtures of Romans and Goths had left it; they departed leaving a great prosperous country teeming with beneficent industries, a paradise of luxury, wealth, and beauty, but sown, alas! with the seeds whose rank and noxious growth has choked to death successive nations.

The present century opens with a war with Portugal which results in no good to either nation, as is usually the case with European wars, attended as they are with so much suffering and bloodshed, to say nothing of the enormous expense of armies and munitions. Then comes Napoleon from Corsica and overturns the world, a feeble world indeed to be so unhinged, and held prostrate under this little boot-heel. But to the disgraceful treaty of Fontainebleau Spain must submit; French troops are sent to the peninsula, and brother Joseph becomes king of Spain. After Bonaparte's disaster in Russia, Spain is relieved of French troops, or rather the French are driven by Wellington across the Pyrenees. Attempts to recover the revolted American colonies fail; Florida is sold to the United States for $5,000,000; external wars and internal revolutions continue to occupy attention, and still the wheels of destiny revolve.

The glory of Spain has indeed departed. Why is it so? Will it ever return? The conditions are plainly to be seen; the cause is not difficult to trace; as to the future, the question can best be answered with the answer to other questions. Will the glory of Egypt ever return? When the West shall have become as old as now is the East, will the East then have renewed its youth and be sending antiquarians to study the monuments of the West? Look at Andalusia as it is to-day, a region that has ever been the garden of Spain, in every respect favored of heaven, with soil still so rich that it enriches man with but little care or labor. Along the banks of the Guadalquiver were once 12,000 smiling villages; there are now less than 800. Extensive irrigation and drainage canals constructed by the Arabs have been allowed to go to ruin. In other places the contrast between the present and the past is still more striking, a sterile soil, marsh lands, and miasmas taking the place of productive and populous areas.

Spain's greatness came through the shaping of great events by great men, who nevertheless hindered as well as aided progress. Prince Henry of Portugal and the Genoese sailor did more for Spain than Charles V and his son Philip; yet these monarchs were great as compared with those who succeeded them, though hampering themselves with follies and fanaticisms such as were eventually to undermine the stability of the state. With the expulsion of the Moors and Jews, Ferdinand and Isabella deprived Spain of her best artisans, farmers, and men of business. When Philip and his successors restricted the traffic of the colonies to dealings with the mother country, under the infatuation that to deluge the land with American gold was to establish therein the foundations of wealth and grandeur, they were merely sowing the dragon's teeth of luxury and laziness which were to stifle industry, crush out commerce and transfer to England those industries which aided in making her one of the greatest of nations. The short-sighted policy of these rulers over many peoples left to the nation itself no people, no men of brawn and brain to give support to the non-working aristocracy on the one hand and the non-working beggars on the other, no tiers etat, or middle class, made substantial and respectable by intelligence, labor, and economy, such as is to be found in the more progressive of European countries.

While Spain was laying under tribute islands and continents before unknown, but abounding in wealth of precious metals, precious stones, and all the products of tropic and temperate climes, was creating new and unlimited markets for the cloths of Segovia, the leather of Cordova, the blades of Toledo, and the silks of Seville, her military and political power were such as to make all the world tremble. Eight centuries of fighting at home and abroad, with all the hardening effects of war and self-denial, had made strong the arm of the nation, soon to become weak and nerveless under boundless prosperity. Commerce and manufactures were the first to vanish, and then the dominion itself. Spain was ruined by gold, while in Mexico and Peru adventurers perpetrated in her name atrocities and treacheries such as should make Satan blush, yet sanctioned by Spain which pocketed greedily the reward. The gold-laden galleons from the New World fed the lust of wealth and spread moral and industrial disease throughout the peninsula. Then there were the iniquitous tax of mortmain, the licensed monopolies in favor of the nobility, and the system of migratory flocks and herds which ruined agriculture, all uniting to destroy commerce and manufactures. As a natural sequence what could be expected but social, industrial, and political decadence, a retrogression in art, literature, and intellectual refinement? Here is probably the true reason that all efforts at a republican form of government have proved abortive; for such a government requires an intelligent and dependent middle class, a factor ever missing in the body politic of Spain.

Portugal, the Lusitania of the Romans, was early visited by the Phoenicians, Carthaginians, and Greeks for purposes of trade with the ancient Celtic tribes. In political and international affairs it has usually followed the fortunes of Spain, being sometimes an integral part of that monarchy and sometimes independent. In common with the rest of the world, this country has its attractions, and though poorer than some, it is by no means the poorest of European countries. Lisbon, with its hills and vales, is one of the most picturesque of cities. The praco de Rocio, the praco de Commercio, and praco de Ouro, or place of Gold, are spacious plazas with beautiful public buildings, the second named with one side open to the river. Of striking appearance, occupying the highest point of the city, is the citadel of St. George. The old prisons of the inquisition in the praco de Rocio are now fitted up as offices of the ministry. Besides the residences of the nobility and rich merchants, the basilicas of San Roque and the Coracas de Jesus present an imposing appearance, as do the royal palaces of Ajuda Bemposta and Nesessidades. Outside the city, on the bank of the Tagus, is the monastery of Belem, built by king Emanuel in 1499, and whose site marks the spot whence Vasco da Gama embarked on the voyage which resulted in the Portuguese occupation of the

MONASTERY, BELEM

Indies. At Evora, the capital of Alemtejo, are Roman antiquities, including a temple of Diana, the present money value of which it were difficult to determine, though doubtless worth something to see and talk about.

Oporto is famous throughout the world for its export of good wine, as a seaport, and as a city of churches. It is built along and back from the banks of the river, and occupies also the slopes of two hills as far as their summits, presenting a pleasing appearance. A quay, two miles in length, also extends along the river. Of eleven public squares the praco de Constituicao and the campo de Cordaria are the largest. Eighty churches, built at various times, are still in existence, while fifteen convents are used for secular purposes. A large

OPORTO

suspension bridge attracts notice; also the hospital and various manufactures. Braga has some antiquities; at Guimaraens is made cutlery and linen, and at Lima are fishing industries, though these might be largely and profitably increased were the people so inclined, for the people of Lima are lacking in enterprise, in common with most of their countrymen.

The Romans held Portugal from B.C. 140 until the coming of the Visigoths in the fifth century, the latter being disturbed in their possession by the Arabs, and these yielding finally to Alfonso of Leon and Castile, whose grandson founded the kingdom of Portugal in 1139. By his son and successor Dom Sancho I, the Moors were further humiliated, and the nation raised to wealth and power, which reached its climax under John I, who died in

1433. It is said that at this time there were no people in Europe more enlightened or enterprising than the Portuguese. Under the energetic rule of Prince Henry, son of John I and properly surnamed the Great, arose the spirit of enterprise which prepared for Columbus the path of discovery, and rested not until all the world was laid open to European civilization. The more immediate results of the prince's efforts were the expansion of geographical knowledge, and carrying forward explorations along the African coast, extended during the reign of Dom Emanuel the Fortunate in the voyage round the cape of Good Hope by Vasco da Gama. Assuming the supremacy in the Indian ocean, by judicious management Portugal was enabled to maintain her hold for nearly a century on all that was best worth

VASCO DA GAMA

possessing on the southern coast of Asia and the eastern coast of Africa. Through the discovery of Brazil by a Portuguese navigator in 1501, she also dominated this vast section of South America for more than 300 years.

In due time came the inevitable decline. In the government the weak succeeded the strong, and the feeble-minded took the place of the wise. Philip II seized the crown upon the death of Dom Henry in 1580 without direct heirs, and for sixty years the yoke of Spain was worn. Then arose revolt, followed by a long war, and Portugal was again free. The French under Napoleon held the country in 1807, until expelled by Wellington's forces, since which time the spirit of insurrection has not been idle.

Portugal has a population of from three and a half to four millions, though except Lisbon and Oporto there are no cities having more than 20,000 inhabitants. There is much good soil but it is poorly cultivated, owing to the thriftlessness of the people and imperfect implements of husbandry. Citrons, almonds, peaches, figs, and melons spring from the ground spontaneously; wheat, wine, and olives are staples products; and corn-meal bread and goat's milk the common food of the people. Hemp and flax are grown, likewise sugar cane and rice; all the fruits are raised abundantly, and of trees there are the cork, bay, licorice, chestnut, myrtle, laurel, and others. Gold and silver were mined during the Roman occupation, and even now a little gold is taken from the beds and banks of streams. There are hot and mineral springs with reputed healing waters; coal and iron are plentiful; copper exists near Oporto and cinnabar at Couna, besides which lead, antimony, and plumbago are found in places. Great quantities of salt are exported, and there are quarries of marble, limestone, and other minerals, with beds of porcelain clay. Of the $40,000,000 estimated as the annual value of agricultural products, wine is placed at $12,000,000, grain at $10,000,000, and wool at $7,000,000. Most of the manufacturing is done at Lisbon, and as a rule not on a very large scale. Among the articles produced are cotton and woollen cloths, pottery and porcelain, iron and tin ware, jewelry and silk, glass and paper. Transportation facilities have never been good, poor roads, the absence of canals, and the obstructions in the streams uniting with the general indolence and apathy of the people as barriers to progress and prosperity.

The nobility and aristocracy of Lisbon have their villas in the suburbs, beyond which are picturesque farms and vineyards. The summer they often spend at Cintra, a dozen miles away, near where the Tagus meets the sea. The latter is approached under long arcades of trees, through which appear orchards of lemons and gardens of myrtle and fuchsias. Here on a terraced mountain-side overlooking the ocean is the Portuguese Alhambra, palace prison and church, built originally by Moorish sultans, completed by Dom Joas I and Dom Manuel, and occupied with equal pleasure by Moslem and Christian. A clustered pile covering an entire hill, with its mixed Arabian and Portuguese buildings, it is more striking at first view than the Alhambra of Granada. Stretches of deep green verdure are broken by buildings of conventual appearance, the common court being entered by a large gateway and the palace by a flight of stairs. The interior is not gorgeous, though some

CINTRA

of the rooms are brilliant in many colors, and in one is a marble mantel fashioned by Michael Angelo. In the palace are the hall of Swans, the hall of Magpies, and the hall of Stags; a garden blooms on the hillside, the entire surface of which is watered by fountains and artificial streams, some of the former with imposing figures and columns. Not far distant is Mafra, the Escurial of Portugal, once a palace and mausoleum, with marble clocks and bells, with hundreds of rooms and several thousand doors.

Finally it may be said that in Portugal, as well as in Spain, while Christian sovereigns have not been idle in the prosecution of great works, to the Arabs are due the finest monuments significant of wealth, learning, luxury, and refinement.

When in 1432 Portugal took possession of the Azores or Western islands, they were uninhabited, and even now contain only about 200,000 people, who cultivate sugar-cane, coffee, and various fruits, exporting oranges and lemons, coarse linen, salted beef, and pork, wine and brandy.

Madeira was occupied by the Portuguese several years before they laid claim to the

GARDEN IN MADEIRA

Azores. The island was then well wooded; hence the name, madeira, or as in Latin, materia, signifying timber. It has a luxurious climate, world-famous for its healing qualities, though not superior to that of California and other health resorts. In the way of agriculture, mining, or manufactures, the 80,000 or 90,000 inhabitants have little to boast of. After wine, for four centuries the chief article of export, comes the cultivation of cochineal, introduced as an industry upon the failure of the grape crop from disease in 1852. The isle is rugged, its geologic formation being little else than basaltic rock; but the scenery is grand, the annual rainfall being about 30 inches, and the mercury ranging from 46 to 80°. From a soil not over exuberant, walled in places and terraced to prevent its being washed into the sea, grow, besides the usual grains and vegetables, sugar-cane, arrow-root, and coffee; also nearly every kind of fruit common to temperate climes, together with the orange, fig, guava, mango, pine-apple, and mulberry. Walnuts are common, and in the mountains are chestnuts, furnishing food for the people. There are no land mammals indigenous to Madeira; but domesticated animals have been introduced to a small extent by the Portuguese, while manufactures consist only of coarse linen and woollen cloth, of straw hats, baskets, and shoes.

The Canaries, supposed to be the Fortunate islands of the elder Pliny, Plutarch, and Ptolemy were early occupied by Spain, and have now a population of some 260,000 Spaniards, whose complexions are somewhat darker than with others of their countrymen, either through exposure to the sun, or intermixture with the aboriginal Guanches, now extinct. On the fertile soil are raised in profusion the products of

GRAND CANARY ISLAND

both temperate and tropic zones, among them grain, vegetables, fruits, and tobacco, while of silk and olive oil the yield is also considerable. Until 1853, prior to the grape disease, wine and brandy were largely exported, but the loss has been more than compensated by the introduction of cochineal. Hats and baskets are made of the leaves of the date-palm, and coarse linen silk and woollen fabrics are manufactured for home use.

On the Cape Verde islands, occupied by some 15,000 Portuguese, flourish all the fruits of southern Europe and western Africa, while indigo grows wild. Goats and fowls are prolific, and asses are raised for exportation to the West Indies.

The Balearic islands have been occupied at various times by the Phoenicians, the Rhodians, and the Carthaginians, not to mention the Romans, Vandals, Goths, and Moors, finally becoming an integral part of the kingdom of Spain. The inhabitants number about 275,000. The soil is fertile and the climate salubrious. The chief products of Majorca and Minorca are grains, fruits, vegetables, and oil, and in the former is a considerable yield of wine and brandy. Both manufacture to a small extent, and in both are profitable live-stock industries. Ivica is the most productive among the group, but with a scattered and somewhat indolent population.

MISCELLANY. — According to the census taken in 1887, the population of Spain, which since that time has increased but slightly, was 17,565,632, or an average of 88 to the square mile, against 10,061,480 in 1789. At the former date the sexes were about equally divided, but with a slight preponderance of females. Nearly 5,000,000 were engaged in agriculture; less than 250,000 in manufactures, and in trades and arts more than 800,000. There were only five cities with over 100,000 inhabitants, — Madrid, Barcelona, Valencia, Seville, and Malaga, Madrid having 470,000 people, Barcelona 272,000, and the others from 171,000 to 134,000.

In 1889 more than 68 per cent of the population could neither read nor write, and this notwithstanding an elaborate system of primary schools, with compulsory education, at least in name. This may be due in part to the small pay of teachers in the primary grades, ranging from $50 to $100 a year. In the budget for 1887 the total sum appropriated to educational purposes was only $355,000, schools being mainly supported by municipalities, which for 1894 contributed in all nearly $5,000,000, or about one-fourth of the sum expended for like purposes in the single state of New York.

Since time immemorial the finances of Spain have been in a disorganized condition, Charles III for instance increasing what was before a heavy national debt to $250,000,000, while under Ferdinand VII the expenditure was $87,500,000, against $50,000,000 of revenue. For four out of the six years ending with 1893 the public outlay exceeded the income, the expenditure for 1892-3 being $144,000,000 and the revenue $134,500,000. In 1893 the Spanish debt, reduced in amount and consolidated a few years before, by consent of the parties interested, into a series of four per cent bonds, exceeded $1,000,000,000, with floating and other indebtedness, including $570,000 due the United States, but never, as it would seem, to be paid, amounting in all to nearly $200,000,000.

In case of war, an army of nearly 1,000,000 men can be mobilized, the regular forces mustering on a peace footing about 120,000 and the remainder consisting of the active and sedentary reserves, though many of these exist only on paper. There are 13 military schools and all over 19 years of age are liable to conscription. In 1893 there were 97 vessels in the Spanish navy, including those in course of construction. Of these only one, the Pelayo, of 9,900 tons displacement, would be ranked by other powers as a battleship; but in Spain heavily armored cruisers are counted as such. There were nine cruisers of the first class, six of the second, and 46 of the third, with two coast-defence vessels and 33 torpedo boats. The number of seamen was 14,000, and of marines 9,000, the total annual expense of army and navy amounting to nearly $30,000,000.

There are probably at the present day in Spain not less than 3,500,000 landed proprietors and tenant farmers, the number being largely increased within recent years, thus

WINE-MAKING

giving hopeful prospects to agricultural industries. Their holdings are small for the most part, some paying no more than one real, or twelve cents, a year as land tax, and at least 1,000,000 paying less than 20 reals. About 80 per cent of the soil is classed under agricultural and grazing lands, with cereals fruits, pulse, flax, and hemp as the leading crops. But the vine is of more importance than all the rest; for in 1890 more than 5,000,000 acres were devoted to viticulture, producing 640,000,000 gallons of wine, in addition to an enormous quantity of raisins and table grapes. While the yield has since been greatly diminished by disease, it is still on a very considerable scale.

In 1894 no less than 5,000 Spanish mines were registered; but of these not more than 2,000 were worked, the total value of all metallurgical products falling little short of $40,000,000. Iron, copper, lead, and quicksilver are the products of most economic value, the ores being largely exported in addition to those which are used for home manufacture. Of iron ore the yield is estimated at 5,500,000 tons; of copper ore 3,500,000, and of lead and argentiferous galena the output is valued at $13,000,000, while the mining industries of Spain are sufficient to give employment to 50,000 or 60,000 men, they are as yet but partially developed; for except as to coal, Spain is probably the richest mineral country in Europe, and one of the richest in the world.

The total of Spanish exports for 1893 amounted to $120,000,000, and of imports to $130,000,000, showing in both cases a reduction of nearly 30 per cent since 1890, due mainly to the decrease in exports of wine from $60,000,000 in the latter year to $21,0000,000 in the former. It is worthy of note that more than 60 per cent of the wines exported from Spain are marketed in France, herself one of the largest wine producing countries in the world; but this is probably for admixture with lighter wines, as with those of California, which after being subjected to French manipulation sell at from three to five times their former price. Next among exports in order of value are iron, copper, and lead, in the ore or manufactured; cottons and woollens; animals and animal products; fruits and timber. Wheat is largely imported; for in common with those of most European countries the crops of Spain do not suffice for home consumption. Raw cotton and wool, coal and coke, wood and wooden ware, drugs and chemicals, tobacco and cigars, machinery and other forms of manufacture figure hugely among the imports. The bulk of Spanish commerce is with France, Great Britain, and the Spanish colonies, traffic with all other countries being in comparison of small amount.

In June 1894 the Banco de Esparta held gold and silver to the amount of $81,000,000, with deposits of $67,000,000 and a note circulation of $170,000,000, the only paper money issued in Spain. With the rehabilitation of the national credit, caused by a reduction in the capital and interest of the public debt, the standing of the bank has been greatly improved; for it is not very long since its bills were refused in the financial centres of Europe.

The monetary system is founded on that of France, the peseta, which is the unit of value, being the exact equivalent of a franc, with gold coins of 5, 10, and 20, and silver coins of 5 and single peseta pieces.

The merchant marine consisted in 1894 of 760 vessels, of which more than one-half were steamers, with a tonnage of 450,000, that of the sailing ships, including smaller craft, being less than 100,000. Entrances for 1893 were 16,200 vessels of 11,450,000 tons, with clearances of about equal amount, nearly one-half of the vessels carrying the Spanish flag.

At the beginning of the present century there were not 500 miles of carriage or wagon road in all the kingdom; in 1894 there were more than 30,000 miles. In 1848 was opened the first of Spanish railways, a distance of 17 miles, from Barcelona to Mataro. A few years later railroad

TRAVEL AND TRANSPORTATION

building was undertaken on a considerable scale; so that about 7,000 miles are now opened for traffic. All are the property of companies and corporations; but with few exceptions they have received grants or guarantees of interest from the government, to which the various lines would revert after a term of 99 years. There are about 20,000 miles of telegraph lines, and nearly 3,000 post-offices, with an efficient postal system.

Nearly one-half of the surface of Portugal is useless for agricultural or other purposes, though there are several million acres of good farm lands yet uncultivated. Mineral wealth is abundant; but coal and wood are scarce, and hence many valuable mines remain untouched. About 6,000 men and nearly 1,000 females, many of the latter under 16 years of are age, are employed in iron, copper, antimony, manganese, lead, and other mining, a large percentage of the products being exported. Factories are few, and apart from agriculture less than 100,000 persons are engaged in Portuguese industries.

In the main commerce has steadily increased in Portugal within the last 30 or 40 years, imports for 1890 exceeding $60,000,000 and exports $37,000,000. For 1893 the figures show a decline of about 20 per cent in the former and 10 or 12 per cent in the latter. With Spain legitimate traffic is small, not more than $4,000,000 or $5,000,000 a year; but there is probably twice that amount of smuggling. With England the trade is considerable, and next, in the order named, are Germany, France, Brazil, the United States, and Belgium. As in Spain, cereals are largely imported, and wine is the chief article of export, more than 3,000,000 gallons being shipped in 1893 to Great Britain alone, and this the smallest shipment for several years. From $14,600,000 in 1888, the value of Portuguese wines shipped to all countries fell to $8,800,000 in 1894. For this the phylloxera is chiefly to blame, destroying yearly hundreds of vineyards, and many thousands in all, with disastrous results to the people, who had thrown into this industry their energy and wealth, to the neglect of grain and other farming.

Portugal has money, the bank of Portugal holding in June 1894 nearly $11,000,000 in coin, and having notes in circulation to the amount of $57,000,000, while other banks, to the number of 37, had in 1890 $16,000,000 in specie, $13,800,000 in notes, and $40,000,000 in deposits. Nevertheless the monetary system is somewhat deranged, the notes of the national bank being mainly used as a circulating medium.

As with Spain, the public indebtedness of Portugal has grown within recent years, until it has become almost unmanageable, amounting to $480,000,000 in 1890. Then came a reduction of interest, but not of the principal, which kept on increasing until in 1894 it exceeded $700,000,000, a heavy burden in truth for a population of less than 5,000,000 and so poor that few can afford an education, and 80 per cent can neither read nor write. It is many a long year since the revenue balanced the expenditure, the deficit being met by borrowing, and hence the frightful incubus of debt. Of late, however, vigorous efforts have been made to reduce the outlay, and for 1893-4 the revenue and expenditure, as estimated at least, were about the same, the latter being a little over $50,000,000, against $64,000,000 for 1891-2. Of the former sum $5,700,000 was to be expended in maintaining an army of 34,000 men, apart from reserves, and $3,500,000 to be spent on a navy of 45 vessels, great and small.

The railway mileage in Portugal is about 1,600, most of the lines belonging to the state and the remainder receiving subsidies. In the kingdom itself there are probably 5,000 miles of telegraph lines, and a submarine cable laid between Lisbon and Rio de Janeiro affords communication between the mother country and her former colony.

Spain's possessions on the African coast, including the Chafarinas and Alhucemas islands, the ports of Melilla and Penon de Velez, are mainly used as convict stations.

Returning to the ancient days of Spain may first be mentioned the familiar but somewhat doubtful story as to the men of Saguntum, when their city was about to fall into the hands of Hannibal. It is said that making a great fire in the public square, they threw into it first their gold and silver and then themselves. How much of the metal the conquerors recovered, history does not record.

Early in the annals of Toledo, the Jews, by whom indeed it is said that city was founded, became very rich; so king Wamba robbed them and drove them out of the country. This was in the seventh century, and long before and ever since that date, even to the present decade, the Jews have been constantly liable to confiscation of property and exile. One would think that if it is a righteous and politic measure to rob them, they might be allowed to remain in the country, if only to gather more gold and be robbed again.

When the Spaniards took Toledo from the Moors they taxed every Jew 30 pieces of silver, the price at which Christ was sold. In one year, that of 1492, there were driven from Spain by Ferdinand and Isabella 170,000 Hebrews.

Not satisfied with burning Jews and Arabs, Ximenes destroyed books, those otherwise imperishable instructors of mankind. Thousands of Arabic manuscripts, particularly such as related to theology, the worthy bishop committed to the flames.

Pedro the Cruel, coveting the wealth of his faithful adherent Samuel Levi the Jew, who built the synagogue called El Transito, in Toledo, was not content to take from him his wealth without cause, but first tortured him and then put him to death.

The cathedral at Toledo has a collection of church vestments which are something wonderful in the way of art needlework,

GALLERY, PEDRO EL CRUEL

probably the finest specimens in existence of the beauty and magnificence of which that art is capable. In the Virgin's wardrobe is a mantle having embroidered in it 78,000 pearls, besides countless diamonds, rubies, and emeralds.

The Generalife in Granada now belongs to the family of Grimaldi in Genoa. At Hinadamar, not far from Granada, is a Carthusian convent famous for the beauty of its marbles, jaspers, and inlaid ebony and tortoise-shell.

At Granada one of the first European postal systems was organized by the Moors, and partly on that system was based the one established in France by Louis XI.

There were once in Salamanca 25 churches, 25 convents, 25 colleges having each 25 professors, and a bridge with 25 arches. The bridge alone remains intact. In the library of Salamanca is a book containing the Lord's prayer in 157 languages. The first gold brought from America by Columbus was given out of gratitude to the convent of the Dominicans in this city to gild the retablo of their church.

In one of the sacristies of the Burgos cathedral is the traditional chest which the Cid filled with stone and sand, with a top layer of gold and gems, for the purpose of borrowing money from two wealthy Jews, to whom he displayed what purported to be a great mass of treasure. He succeeded in his purpose.

COFRE DE EL CID

The Moslem monarch Abderrahman I, when he had established himself in Spain, demanded as tribute 10,000 ounces of gold, 10,000 pounds of silver, 10,000 horses, 10,000 mules, and 1,000 cuirasses. In the cathedral of Cordova, originally built as a mosque for this sovereign, the pillars, still nearly 700 in number, though many have been destroyed, are of jasper, marble, and porphyry in many tints, forming one of the finest specimens of mosaic work belonging to the Moorish period.

When Abderrahman III reigned at Cordova, he was called the richest monarch in the world; by systems of irrigation agriculture was developed; commerce, science, and art were at their best, and millions of gold pieces filled his coffers, most of which he expended on public works.

Mary, infanta of Portugal, was but fifteen years of age when she came to Spain to marry Philip II who was sixteen. She sat gracefully upon her mule, on a silver saddle, gowned in silver cloth embroidered with gold, and a velvet hat with white and blue plumes. To obtain a good look at her without himself being known, Philip mingled in disguise among the crowd. On the eve of his second marriage, — with bloody Mary — he was about to he mobbed, but the wrath of the people was somewhat quieted by the appearance of cart loads of Mexican and Peruvian silver, which were rolled on before him.

Never was such a gift from father to son, or from one man to another, as that made by Charles V, when 56 years old, to Philip II, then 29. In territory, wealth, and other possessions the gift fell not far short of half the world, and what it contains. Besides Spain and Spanish America, there were Franche-Comte and the Netherlands, Naples and Sicily, and other vast areas in Europe, Asia, and Africa.

Eleven archbishops and 62 bishops controlled one-third of the Spanish revenue during the time of Philip II. The clerical class in Spain in 1749 comprised 182,000 persons, of whom 112,000 were in orders, the annual income of the church at this time was not less than 359,000,000 reals.

In Spain, as elsewhere, rulers have often become rich by questionable means, Queen Christina, for instance, making, it is said, $40,000,000 by speculating in stocks. And so with officials; one class acquiring wealth by smuggling; another through bribery, a third through blackmail; the assessors being probably as honest and thrifty as any, unless it was the judges.

There is a royal jewel of Spain, an opal surrounded by diamonds, as unlucky as it is valuable. No less than five owners have died within 20 years, Alfonso XII, who gave it to his cousin Mercides, on her death going to Queen Christina, then to the Infanta del Pilar, then to Christina, daughter of the duke of Montpensier. It was finally hung round the neck of the virgin of Almudena, where let us hope it is powerless for evil.

The people of Spain support, besides the royal family, 96 dukes, 900 marquises, 750 counts, 130 viscounts, 76 barons, and 243 grandees, with their relatives and retainers.

The young king of Spain has a civil list of $1,500,000 a year; his mother $100,000, his sister $100,000; the ex-queen Isabella, $15,000; and her husband $600,000.

Doubtless the story of the Invincible Armada sounds sweeter to English than to Spanish ears, though the shame of defeat adds little lustre to the good fortune of success. The preparations of Philip for the invasion of England were completed in May, 1588.

Sixty-five of the 130 vessels were large ships and galleons; there were 25 smaller ships, 19 tenders, 4 galleasses, and 4 galleys. The soldiers numbered 19,295, mariners 8,050, and rowers 2,088. Of this force Portugal supplied 4,623 men. On board the fleet were 2,431 pieces of artillery and 4,575 quintals of powder. Besides the regular soldiers 2,000 volunteers, belonging to the most aristocratic families in Spain, accompanied the expedition. A formidable force was likewise prepared in the Netherlands. The duke of Parma, with 30,000 foot and 4,000 horse in the vicinity of Nieuport and Dunkirk, awaited the

DUKE OF PARMA

arrival of the Spaniards, flat-bottomed boats, built for the most part at Antwerp, and conveyed by river and canal in order to avoid the English vessels which guarded the coast, being ready to transport the troops to British shores.

Queen Elizabeth made ready to meet the foe on sea and land, — on sea with 181 ships and 17,472 men, on land with two armies, one under the earl of Leicester, of 18,449 men to move immediately upon the enemy, the other of 45,362 men under Lord Hunsdon to defend the person and possessions of the queen. There were also forces in the north and west to prevent inroads from Scotland or Wales, should any such be attempted.

QUEEN ELIZABETH

Ill luck attended Philip's efforts from the beginning. First, on the eve of departure, the Marques de Santa Cruz, who had been appointed admiral of the Armada, sickened and died, as did also the vice-admiral, the duke of Paliano, — both able officers, at whose sudden and singular demise suspicions of foul play were entertained. The vacant posts were filled as quickly as possible, the first by the duke de Medina Sidonia, a nobleman of high repute but with little knowledge of maritime warfare, the other by Martinez de Recaldo, an able and experienced captain.

Setting sail from Lisbon on the 29th of May, the fleet was dispersed by a storm, all but four of the ships, however, reaching Corunna, where they were delayed several weeks undergoing repairs. The report reached England that the Armada was destroyed, whereupon the queen ordered her secretary to instruct Lord Howard, the English admiral, to lay up four of his largest ships and discharge the seamen. But the admiral begged that he be first allowed to prove the truth of the rumor, offering himself to bear the cost of the delay. Sailing for the coast of Spain, he found that the Armada was not seriously damaged, and fearing that the Spaniards might reach England before his return, hastened hack to Plymouth, whence he had sailed. Hardly had he cast anchor than he was told that the Armada was in sight; and there indeed it was, in all its imposing, array, sailing through the channel in the form of a crescent, seven miles in length, and making direct for the coast of Flanders, there to meet the duke of Parma.

Not strong enough to attack, the English fleet hovered in the wake of the Spaniards, ready to take advantage of whatever might befall in their favor, Sir Francis Drake capturing two vessels, one of which took fire. The Spaniards labored under a disadvantage in these narrow seas, owing to the size of their vessels and the height of their guns above water. Fire ships were sent against them with good effect; and defeated at every turn, with provisions beginning to fail, they decided to return to Lisbon for fresh supplies, passing around the northern end of the British

SIR FRANCIS DRAKE isles for that purpose. But while rounding the Orkneys a storm struck and scattered the fleet, well-nigh destroying it; the coasts of Scotland and Ireland were strewn with wrecks and the crews were captured by the inhabitants; the duke of Medina, by keeping to the open sea, reaching Santanter toward the end of September with sixty sail.

Thus fails Philip "to serve God, and to return unto his church many contrite souls that are oppressed by the heretics, enemies to our holy catholic faith, which have them subject to their sects," while Elizabeth betakes herself in solemn procession to church, and thanks God for the defeat of Philip's pious plans, extending her hands in blessing on the people in answer to their joyous acclamations.

MANUSCRIPT PHILIP III,
BOOK OF HOURS, ESCURIAL

At the Escurial is shown today the desk at which Philip was writing when Christoval de Moura arrived to tell of the mighty misadventure of an expedition which had cost him eighteen years of careful preparation and a hundred millions of ducats. Calmly he received the announcement, and without the movement of a muscle in his cold, impassive features, "I thank God," he said, "for having given me the means of bearing such a loss without embarrassment and the power to fit out another fleet of equal size. A stream can afford to waste some water when its source is not dried up."

Among the men of the day, interested in greater or less degree in the momentous events at that time transpiring, were Lord Burleigh, master of the robes to Henry VIII and Elizabeth's lord high treasurer; Sir Francis Walsingham, secretary of state; Sir Christopher

Hatton, who danced himself into the office of lord high chancellor; Sir John Hawkins, rear admiral of the fleet; Sir Walter Raleigh, who planned

the colony of Virginia and wrote a history of the world; Sir Martin Frobisher, one of the most distinguished officers who fought against the Armada; the Earl of Essex, first favored and then beheaded by Elizabeth; Sir Thomas Scott, descendant of Baliol, king of Scotland, and commander of the Kentish forces; Sir John Norris, who served the queen in the Netherlands; the earl of Suffolk, an able commander; the earl of Cumberland, or

SIR FRANCIS WALSINGHAM

SIR WALTER RALEIGH

George Clifford, the queen's champion; the earl of Northumberland, who fought the enemies of England in vessels equipped at his own expense; the earls of Devonshire and Salisbury, who fought in ships hired at their own cost; the earl of Monmouth, who was on board the English fleet when the Armada was scattered; the earl of Exeter, who served against the Armada; the earl of Derby, who was mayor of Liverpool at the coming of the Spaniards, and raised a land force from his private

purse; Lord Cobham, one of the commissioners appointed to treat for peace with the duke of Parma at Ostend; the earl of Dorset, who succeeded Burleigh as lord high treasurer; Henry Stanley, another earl of Derby, one of the peers who sat at the trial of the queen of Scots; Cardinal Allen, who urged Philip to undertake the conquest of England; Robert Parsons, a jesuit who

CARDINAL ALLEN

stirred up sedition among the catholics in England, James VI of Scotland, who succeeded to the English throne on the death of Elizabeth in 1603; Lord Maitland, sometime first minister of James; Prince Maurice of

SIR THOS. SCOTT

Nassau, who reduced Spain to the necessity of making peace with the Hollanders; Justinus de Nassau, admiral of the Zeeland fleet; Joos de Moor, vice-admiral, sent to oppose the 30,000 troops under the duke of Parma; Henry III of France, whose

kingdom was too much distracted to allow him to help Spain against England; Henry IV, who succeeded as king of France and Navarre in 1589; Henri duc de Guise, who advised the massacre of St Bartholomew; Henri de Guzman Olivares, viceroy of Spain; Pope Sixtus V, who purged Rome of outlaws, and while frowning upon the over-reaching ambition of Philip, excommunicated Elizabeth, urged the despatch of the Armada, and promised pecuniary aid for the subjugation of England.

HENRY, DUKE OF GUISE

JUSTINUS DE NASSAU

Then there were William Shakespeare, Miguel de Cervantes Saavedra, et alii eis similes, but whose names are hardly to be mentioned in such worshipful company.

CHAPTER THE NINTH

THE TURKISH EMPIRE

Gold! gold! gold! gold!
Bright and yellow, hard and cold,
Molten, graven, hammered and rolled;
Heavy to get, and light to hold;
Hoarded, bartered, bought, and sold,
Stolen, borrowed, squandered, doled;
Spurned by the young, but hugged by
the old
To the very verge of the church-yard
mould;

Price of many a crime untold:
Gold! gold! gold! gold!
Good or bad a thousand-fold!
How widely its agencies vary -
To save - to ruin - to curse - to bless -
As even its minted coins express,
Now stamped with the image of good
Queen Bess,
And now of a Bloody Mary.

ACCORDING to the chronicler Aboulgazi Bahdur-Khan, the Turks are descended from the eldest son of Japhet and of Mongolian origin; "but," says this historian of his country, "as in gazing on the sun the eye becomes dazzled with its brightness, so does the mind become confused with the brilliant origin of this illustrious race." Belonging to the great Turanian family the Turks spread northward as far as the banks of the Lena and westward into Asia Minor and the shores of the Black sea. Under the name of Tukin, whence probably comes the word Turks, they formed an empire on the borders of the Chinese, by whom they were first defeated and with whom they were afterward united. Then came a division, some of the tribes becoming slaves to the khan of Geougen, and working in the gold-bearing mountains of Altai, or as makers of weapons of war. The remainder formed a nation of warrior-shepherds, with pasture lands of almost unlimited extent, horses forming their principal wealth; so that in one of their armies were 400,000 cavalry. In later times, from the Trebizond, Caucasus, and Altai mines came a steady stream of gold, which metal became so abundant as to be used for the furniture of the earlier emperors, one of whom sat enthroned in a chariot of gold supported by golden peacocks. In the seventh century

Mohammed appears on the scene, his religion spreading with such marvellous rapidity that the converts of Islam far outnumbered those of the Christian faith. About the end of the

tenth century the title of sultan was conferred on Mahmoud, one of the most powerful of Turkish potentates, whose domains extended into Persia and Hindostan. In the reign of Sultan Soliman Turkish troops first landed in Europe as a reinforcement to the Byzantine army at Scutari. Presently began the crusades, notwithstanding which the Turks made good their footing in Europe and Asia Minor, though it was not until the middle of the fifteenth century that they became masters of the long coveted prize on the shore of the Bosphorus.

SCUTARI, ANCIENT QUARTER

Originally a Greek settlement, Constantinople, or Byzantium as first it was called, was founded about the middle of the seventh century of the pre-Christian era, and after being destroyed by one of the satraps of Darius was recolonized by Pausanias. Through its position on the Bosphorus it acquired control of the corn trade between the west and the cities on the Euxive, and from its wealth in tunny and other fisheries its curved bay was named the Golden Horn. Conquered by the Macedonians, it afterward became subject to Rome, and for espousing the cause of her enemies was demolished, and later in part rebuilt by Severus. By Constantine was reared a new city more than double the size of its predecessor, and enclosed with two walls on the building of which 40,000 Goths were employed, these fortifications being strengthened and repaired by successive rulers until they were believed to be impregnable. They were in three tiers, each higher than the one in front, with towers at intervals of 150 feet, the entire work containing more masonry than

CONSTANTINOPLE

would suffice for all the castles on the Rhine, while the remains are probably the most imposing ruins in the world. There is also a deep, wide foss, now used as a vegetable garden, and separated by open cisterns formerly filled with water sufficient to supply 1,000,000 people during a four months' siege.

At the opening of the thirteenth century Constantinople had become the principal city of the western world, not only as the residence of the emperor and his court, of the wealthy and noble who found in this new Rome all the luxury of the Augustan era, but as the highway of commerce between Europe and Asia, while much even of the traffic of Egypt passing into the Golden Horn. In this treasure-house of the nations had been amassed the riches of many centuries, men who had become wealthy in other lands flocking to the eastern capital to spend or invest accumulations gathered in cities themselves renowned for wealth. The warehouses were filled with gold and silver, with silks and purple cloths, while the citizens lived and attired themselves like princes, their garments glittering with gold and precious stones. Of the palace of Blachernae, fronting on a square where were the statue of Justinian and the silver image of the empress Eudoxia, the walls and columns were covered with gold, and in its golden throne and golden crown were gems of priceless value. "There was gold and silver for all," declares one of the crusaders, "there were vessels of the precious metals, silk and satin cloths, furs of various kinds, and goods of all descriptions that have ever been found or made on the face of the earth." "As to places of worship," says Benjamin of Tuleda, a Spanish Jew sojourning in Constantinople, "all others in the world would not equal in wealth the church of the Divine Wisdom. It was ornamented with pillars of gold and silver and with innumerable lamps of the same materials, and its riches could not be counted." Notwithstanding the strength of their fortifications, no wonder that the inhabitants trembled for the safety of possessions coveted not only by the Turks but by many European monarchs.

The history of Constantinople is in truth little more than a history of its sieges, most famous of which was that which resulted in its capture by Mohammed II. It was then that

MOHAMMED II

artillery first played a prominent part in warfare, a foundry being erected at Adrianople, where, as is said, cannon were cast that would throw a ball 600 pounds in weight. There were also powerful battering-rams and huge engines for hurling stones, while a fleet of ships and an army of 250,000 Turks aided in its work of destruction the grim machinery of death. Long and fierce was the resistance made by the slender garrison of 5,000 men, until in the breach at the gate of St. Romulus the last of the Constantines fell in defence of the city which the first had founded and named. Then came pillage with its nameless horrors, after which the sultan, surrounded with his viziers and pashas who celebrated the triumph of Islam on the high altar of the temple where but a few hours before Christians had prayed for deliverance, calling on their God in deep and earnest supplication, but calling in vain.

"The city and buildings are mine," declared Mohammed; "but I resign to your valor the captives and the spoil, the treasures of gold and beauty." And he kept his word; the booty being gathered by the strongest or by those who were first on the spot, without any attempt at regular division. In all the churches, monasteries, and palaces the work of pillage proceeded without check or hindrance; nor was there any building, however sacred or secluded, that could protect the persons and property of the inhabitants. The church of the Divine Wisdom, where multitudes had taken refuge was despoiled of the offerings of ages in vessels and ornaments of gold and silver, in precious stones, and in sacerdotal vestments, the rapine of a few hours being more productive than the contributions of many centuries. Then the captives, both male and female to the number of 60,000, were driven to the Turkish camp and fleet; the men to be ransomed or sold into slavery, and the virgins to exchange the life of the convent for that of the harem. Not least to be deplored was the destruction of the Byzantine libraries, containing, it is said, 120,000 manuscripts, among which were many of priceless value, ten volumes being offered for a single ducat, while for the same price could be purchased the entire works of Homer and Aristotle.

Among other palatial structures in Constantinople was the imperial palace, the site of which was later occupied by the mosque of Ahmed. It consisted of a series of buildings surrounded with gardens extending in one direction to the hippodrome and in another to the shore of the Golden Horn. Mohammed II erected the palace known as the seraglio in three divisions, one for his guards, one for public receptions, and a third for himself and his household. It became the abode of the Ottoman sultans; but only portions of its walls remain. By Constantine were reared the Palace of the Lord with its coronation hall, better known as the Tekfur-Scrai, at the foot of which is the mosque of Kahrich.

The mosque of St. Sofia, occupying the site of successive Christian churches, is the most imposing of the sacred edifices, and one of the finest specimens of Byzantine architecture. Among the churches was that of the Divine Wisdom, erected by Constantine,

ST. SOFIA

the first dedicated to the new faith, and on a magnificent scale. Destroyed during the Christian schisms, it was reconstructed by Justinian with funds obtained in part by melting a silver statue of himself thirty-seven tons in weight, the total cost exceeding $5,000,000. Ten thousand men were employed on this structure under the personal supervision of the emperor, who paid them every night for their task and bestowed rewards on the more skilful and diligent workmen. It was nearly six years in building, and when it was completed it is said that the emperor, proudly surveying his temple as did Nebuchadnezzar the city which he had built, exclaimed, "I have conquered thee, O Solomon." The exterior is of brick and somewhat crude in design; but within a striking effect is produced by the costly marbles which line the walls and by the bold sweep of the dome, 180 feet in height, resting on massive arches and flanked with colonnades of many-colored pillars supporting lofty galleries. Among the columns, more than 100 in number, are those which Constantine removed from the temples of Apollo at Rome and of Diana at Ephesus. Both walls and dome were encrusted with mosaics in many figures and devices, of which little now remains except the colossal seraphim with wings 50 feet long, their features being obliterated when the church was converted into a mosque. The building has been many times repaired and restored, especially in 1849, when it was found that the dome was too heavy for its supporting walls.

Of the hundreds of mosques and mesjids in Constantinople, many are built not only on the site but with the materials of Christian churches, among them that of Suleiman the Magnificent, with an area of 52,000 square feet, and in dimensions and design resembling

SULTAN ATTENDS MOSQUE

the fane of Saint Sophia, though internally far inferior as to decorative scheme. It is in the form of a Greek cross, surrounded by a quadrangle, as are most of the Turkish mosques, their plan being adopted from Christian models without reference to their origin. The entrance-way is approached by a broad flight of marble steps, and of singular beauty are its lofty pillars of Egyptian porphyry. Most of the hills on which, as in Rome, the city is built are crowned with mosques whose stately domes and minarets stand forth in bold relief, and especially striking is the effect when, illumined by night on festal occasions, they cast on the waters of the Golden Horn festoons of dazzling light.

Of the imperial hippodrome, with its rows of white marble seats resembling those of the Dionysias theatre at Athens, most of the materials were used for the building of mosques. Founded by Severus, it was constructed and adorned by several of the emperors, among its decorations being an obelisk of Egyptian syenite, the pyramid which served as a goal, and the bronze horses now contained in the church of St Mark at Venice. But its most famous monument was the column of the Three Serpents, which formerly supported the golden tripod in the temple of Delphi, captured by the Greeks after the battle of Plataea. Elsewhere in the city and especially around and within the mansions of the rich, thickly clustered in the fashionable quarter, were many columns, statues, and paintings; for Constantinople, like Rome, was a storehouse of Grecian art.

Of secular and especially commercial buildings of the better class, Galata on the northern side of the Horn, built up to the crest of a hill crowned with a ponderous fifth-century tower, is now one of the principal quarters. In former ages, when Constantinople was occupied by the Genoese, the tower was their principal defence, being joined to another huge castle on the opposite shore by a massive iron chain for protection against hostile fleets. Near it are the stores and banks and merchants' offices of the business quarter, not far from which are the palace of the podesta and the Lombard church of St. Benedict. Scutari, though on the Asiatic shore of the Bosphorus, may be regarded as a suburb of Constantinople. It is a beautiful town, built in the form of an amphitheatre on the slopes of several hills, beyond which are gardens, villas, and one of the largest cemeteries in the world, in its centre the great dome with marble pillars erected by Sultan Mohammed in memory of his favorite horse. Connected with Scutari are many historic recollections, its ancient name of Chrysopolis, or the city of

GALATA TOWER

gold, being probably derived from the tribute collected by the Persians, who also formed here a depot for the rich spoils collected from the Greek settlements on the Asiatic coast.

Adrianople, named after the emperor Hadrian, whose improvements gave to it a more pleasing appearance than it now presents, with its narrow tortuous and refuse-littered streets, ranks next to Constantinople in importance. Among its public buildings are the mosque of Selim II, one of the most splendid of Mohammedan edifices, as also was the ancient palace of the sultans now fallen into decay. Bazaars are numerous, chief among them being that of Ali Pasha, and there is a considerable volume of commerce and manufactures in this city of 70,000 people. The country around is extremely fertile; the mines in its neighborhood were formerly among the most productive in the world, and here is the chief source of supply for the great fairs at which merchants gather from all quarters of European Turkey.

Salonica, the Thessalonica of ancient and the Therma of still more ancient days, was an important city more than twenty-five centuries ago, when the plains that surround it were covered with prosperous Macedonian settlements. There the army of Xerxes encamped, and there was the naval station of Macedonia until after his defeat at Pydna. Perseus, the last of its kings, was carried captive to Rome, there to show the people, as Plutarch relates, "what immense sums he had saved and laid up for them." Its wealth was

derived from rich mines in the neighborhood, as well as from the trade and industries of a large population, while culture was combined with opulence, among the spoils most prized by the conqueror, Paulus Aemilius, being the library of the fallen monarch. Later, during Gothic and other invasions, it became the bulwark of Constantinople and of the Roman empire, one of its monuments being the triumphal arch erected in honor of Constantine, while amid mounds of rubbish are the remains of marble palaces, columns, and sarcophagi, beneath which perchance lie buried some of the treasures of Macedonian sovereigns. Still are to be seen the remnants of the white marble portico of the hippodrome where, without regard to age or sex, Theodosius massacred 15,000 persons whom he had treacherously invited to the games. An imposing structure is the castle of the Seven Towers, its domes and minarets rising above the foliage of elm and cypress groves. Near the end of the sixteenth century the cathedral of Saint Sofia, probably erected in the time of Justinian, was converted into a mosque, its dome being still covered with figures in mosaic representing the ascension. The dome of St. George's has also its mosaics, whose subject is a series of saints worshipping in front of temples, the decoration, if such it can be termed, covering its entire surface of more than 7,000 square feet, the largest known specimen of ancient mosaic work.

Turkey is exceedingly rich in resources, though among her fertile plains and valleys are large areas of uncultivated land. Her waterfalls are little utilized; her rivers are filled with obstructions; her harbors as nature made them, and many of her roads impassable for wheeled vehicles. The mountains are covered with merchantable timber, and there are vast

ANCIENT
OBELISK

deposits of coal and iron, copper and lead, almost entirely unheeded, while Thracian princes were made wealthy by mines of gold and silver, now no longer worked but far from being exhausted. In Macedonia are veins of copper and argentiferous galena, and cinnabar is found in the region north of the Balkans. The richest of the silver and lead mines are in Mount. Pelion, where is also an abundance of fuel and water-power. Asia Minor and the islands of the Grecian archipelago were famed for their mineral wealth, and though the yield of their mines declined with the decline of the civilization to which they ministered, there is still an abundance of valuable ores awaiting only the advent of capital and enterprise. As Pliny relates, the riches of the island of Cyprus came largely from their copper mines, while there were also the precious metals, the emerald and agate, malachite, jasper, opals, and the rock crystals held in esteem by the Romans. In Lemnos was also copper; in Thasos gold; in Thessaly gold, silver, and lead, while several of the islands were noted for their precious stones.

In former ages the Turks were noted for their skill in handicraft; but the application of steam to nearly all branches of manufacture has deprived them of this pre-eminence, and they are now almost entirely an agricultural people. At the beginning of the present century the markets of the Levant were stocked with Turkish manufactures, which have now given place to articles of English make. Damascus steel no longer exists; the muslin looms of Scutari and the silk looms of Salonica and Broussa have been idle

ADRIANOPLE

for many years, as also have the cotton looms of Aleppo, while Constantinople, Adrianople, and Bagdad are no longer prominent as manufacturing centres. Thus exports consist almost entirely of raw products, chief among them being cereals and fruits, silk cotton and wool, coffee and olive oil. Imports are mainly of cotton and other textile fabrics, with a total value far in excess of exports, leaving a heavy balance of trade against the country to be met by payments in gold.

In the principality of Bulgaria, including eastern Roumelia, are several cities of historic fame, as Philippopolis, Varna, Shumla, Plevna, Silistria, and others whose annals need not here detain us. As with the Turks, the people are an agricultural community, raising cereals, fruits, and other products, of which there is a considerable surplus for export. For the most, part they own the land which they cultivate, building thereon dwellings of wood and clay, in which as a rule large families are reared; for food is cheap and children are set to work at an early age. A portion of their farms is usually devoted to vineyards and flower gardens, and another portion to pasture, the buffalo being largely used for tillage, though of other live-stock there is a plentiful supply. Timber is abundant and wastefully used; minerals are almost entirely neglected, and highway roads are few and poor, though railways connect the capital city of Sona with European systems by way of Constantinople and Belgrade.

Of ancient and modern Egypt a description has already been given, and of Tripoli and other Turkish possessions in Africa I shall have occasion to speak in a later chapter of this work. Passing to Asiatic Turkey we find there much that is worthy of mention, though rather of historic than of transient interest; for here are many of the great centres of

antiquity, from the city of the Troad to those whose spoils filled to overflowing the treasuries of imperial Rome. Of Troy it may be remarked that while implements and weapons resembling those which Homer describes have been unearthed, there is little to prove or disprove the story of its siege.

CHURCH OF PERGAMUM

Of much greater value are such ruins as those of Pergamum, with its temple of Athena Polias and its great sculptured altar of Zeus Soter, of Palmyra, Baalbec, and Djerach, pointing to Syrian civilization as it existed when in the days of Solomon the first of these cities was a storehouse on the principal highway of commerce. Though now a mere hamlet, Palmyra was at one time the mistress of the east, the emporium for the luxuries of the ancient world, the costly fabrics, the pearls and jewels, the perfumes, spices, and unguents of Arabia, India, and China. Greatest of all its monuments was the temple of the Sun, its courtyard, 750 feet square, lined with colonnades resembling those of Herod's temple, and whence from a triumphal arch adjoining radiated the central avenue of the city. No less imposing are the remains of Baalbec, the Heliopolis of the Greeks, though as

RUINS OF DJERACH

to its origin the classical writers are silent. It is known that its walls were four miles in circuit, while its Great temple, 1,100 feet in length and rich in sculptural and columnar ornaments, was well worthy of its name. Here also was a temple of the sun, of which portions are still preserved, and at it the Circular temple, the smallest of the three but the most finished in design and workmanship. When captured by the Moslems Baalbec was one of the wealthiest cities of Syria, containing many palaces and ancient monuments and well supplied with all that contributes to luxurious living. As ransom were exacted 2,000 ounces of gold and 4,000 of silver, 2,000 silken vests, 1,000 swords, and all the arms of the garrison.

Aleppo succeeded to Palmyra as the emporium of commerce between eastern countries and the Mediterranean seaboard, many traces of its former grandeur remaining in the neighborhood of the modern city. Plundered first by the Saracens and then by the Tartars, it finally passed into possession of the Turks early in the sixteenth century, since which time it has suffered much from earthquakes and pestilence. In 1822 the citadel, many of the mosques, and much of the town were laid in ruins by an earthquake which destroyed more than half its population; then came a recurrence of the plague which not many years before had swept away 60,000 persons, the cholera of 1832 adding to a succession of calamities which culminated in the tumults of 1850, when property to the amount of many millions was destroyed by Moslem fanatics. Before these disasters Aleppo was one of the fairest of Turkish cities, and still its mosques and minarets, its Christian temples of worship, its colleges and libraries, with rows of houses built of freestone on the sides of terraced hills, present from a distance a scene of singular beauty. Its trade is still sufficient to maintain more than a hundred mercantile houses, and among many branches of manufacture are its famous silken and other fabrics, flowered or woven with threads of gold and silver.

Damascus was a place of note even in the days of Abraham, whose steward, Eliezer, was a native of that town, many changes of dynasty occurring from the days when its people were carried away captive by the Assyrians, until finally it fell into the hands of the Turks. Few cities have been so often pillaged; but never were the woes of conquest so dire as after its capture by Tamerlane, "the wild beast" as he is called by Arab chroniclers. Though each one promptly paid the redemption money exacted by the conqueror, a general massacre followed, and of the entire Christian population only a single family escaped. Its stores of wealth and treasures of art were carried away or destroyed; its palaces were burned to the ground, and of its libraries, filled with the writings of the caliphs and of the fathers of the church, hardly a vestige remained.

Among the antiquities of Damascus are Roman gateways, walls founded by Seleucid monarchs, and a castle probably erected by one of the Byzantine emperors. Near

the castle, but surrounded with dwellings and bazaars so as to be almost concealed from view, is the Great mosque, its massive exterior colonnades contrasting with slender Saracenic minarets and arcades. It is 430 feet in length, divided into aisles by rows of Corinthian columns, and surmounted by a dome beneath which, it is said, lies the head of John the Baptist, buried in a golden casket. Among other mosques are the Tekiyeh, built by Sultan Selim for the accommodation of pilgrims, and the Senaniyeh, reared by Senan Pasha, with cloistered court and richly decorated chapels, near which are

MOSQUE, DAMASCUS

the tombs of Saladin and other Saracen princes. Damascus is a city of stately domes and tapering minarets, their gilded crescents rising above terraced roofs and luxuriant foliage,

DAMASCUS

presenting at a distance the appearance of an enchanted realm. For sixty miles around it extend the gardens, vineyards, orchards, and meadows watered by the Abana, of which Naaman said, "Are not Abana and Pharpar, rivers of Damascus, better than all the waters of Israel?" The bazaars are the most famous in the East, though merely rows of open stalls on either side of narrow covered alleys; there are also more pretentious marts called khans, where merchants meet for traffic. Gold and silver ornaments, weapons, silks, and woollens are the chief articles manufactured, and for them there is a considerable foreign demand.

Antioch, founded by Seleucus Nicator as his capital after the partition of the Macedonian empire, became in the days of Antiochus Epiphanes a city second only to  Rome and Alexandria in architectural magnificence. From its citadel and the four quarters adjacent extended to the cypress grove of Daphne, with its temple and colossal statue of Apollo, a line of beautiful villas and gardens several miles in length. Of the city itself the streets and porticos were styled golden, in reference to their gilded and stately columns, the principal thoroughfare, paved with granite, having four parallel rows of pillars, leaving a spacious road in the centre, flanked by arcaded sidewalks. Rivalling the great Roman edifice was the temple of Capitoline Jove, while even more imposing was the church which Constantine founded, its domical roof of enormous size and its interior glistening with golden ornaments and precious stones. A noble structure was the theatre founded by Seleucid kings and completed and enlarged by Roman emperors, several of whom visited this eastern metropolis and added to its public monuments. Over one of its gates were placed by Titus the cherubim taken from the temple at Jerusalem; by Hadrian was built at the grove of Daphne a reservoir in the form of a temple dedicated to the nymphs; by Valens many new buildings were erected, including a forum encircled with basilicas in the centre of which was a lofty column. And thus, except for destructive earthquakes, the city prospered until its capture and pillage by Khosru the Persian in 538, whereafter it fell from its high position as the queen city of the East. Several times Antioch was destroyed by earthquakes, entirely or in part. In 115, during a series of violent shocks lasting for several days, the inhabitants fled the town to escape from falling buildings; the mountains shook and the rivers changed their courses; but most disastrous of all was the catastrophe of 526, when, as is related, a quarter of a million of people lost their lives.

ANTIOCHUS EPIPHANES

Of Sardis, the former capital of the Lydian empire, only its ruins remain, except a cluster of huts occupied by a semi-nomadic tribe. During the reign of Croesus it became the wealthiest and most powerful city of the Orient, and long before that time was the industrial metropolis of the ancient world, coined money being here invented, while as a manufacturing centre it was noted for costly and delicate fabrics. To the treasures stored in Sardis, and to its steady stream of wealth-producing commerce, was probably due the legend of the Pactolus flowing through the market-place over sands abounding in gold.

Of all the rich men of the East there were none who compared with Croesus, whose inherited possessions were increased by conquest and traffic until he came to be regarded as the type of human prosperity. His adversaries and those who sided with them he treated with ruthless severity; later, in the hope of expiating his wrongs, presenting magnificent gifts to the temples of the Greeks on the other side of the Aegean, as well as those which he had pillaged. In the temple of Diana at Ephesus, as Strabo relates, he repaired the damage wrought by the Scythians, donating also its golden oxen and many of its marble columns. Still more lavish were his donations to the Delphic fane of Apollo, from whose oracle he sought response as to the issue of the forthcoming war with Cyrus. First offering in sacrifice 3,000 oxen, he incited a sufficient quantity of gold from which to fashion 116 bricks from three to six hands' breadth long and one in thickness. To these were added a golden lion ten talents in weight, a female figure of gold three cubits in height, with vessels and casks of gold and silver. The oracle responded that if Croesus went to war he should destroy a mighty empire; but the empire proved to be his own; for he was defeated and conducted as a prisoner into the presence of Cyrus, who became master of his capital and all his rich store of treasure. As to the fallen monarch, he was sentenced to be burned alive; but the legend relates that while the flames were ascending his funeral pyre, Cyrus relented, and as some have it the fire was extinguished by a shower sent by Apollo in response to his offerings and supplications.

CROESUS ON THE FUNERAL PYRE

In Ephesus, founded according to its own traditions in the eleventh century before Christ, there was from time immemorial a sanctuary of Diana, around which clustered the most ancient quarter of the town. In the time of Croesus the first great temple was partially built, the splendor of the completed structure being largely due to his gifts, prompted rather by policy than piety, his object being to make of Ephesus an Asiatic rather than a Hellenic city. After its destruction in 356 by Herostratus, whose name would probably have perished but for the decree which forbade its use, it was rebuilt on a still more splendid scale, and later was regarded as the finest specimen of Ionic architecture, ranking among the wonders of the world. All Asia contributed to the cost, its 127 pillars of Parian marble being the gifts of as many kings, while the men of Ephesus gave their money and the women their jewelry, refusing the offer of Alexander the Great, on the night of whose birth the fire occurred, to pay the entire expense on condition that his name be inscribed on the pediment. It was 418 feet in length by 230 in width, many of its external columns, 56 feet in height, being sculptured with figures in relief, the remains of which show that they were of no ordinary workmanship. From floor to roof the entire building was of marble; the walls built of solid blocks faced with brass and silver plates, and the frieze adorned with mythological figures of Theseus, Hercules, and other mythological subjects. For centuries the temple was a rich museum of art and other treasures, Roman emperors vying in munificence with wealthy citizens, one of whom presented a large number of gold and silver images to be carried in the processions. There were figures of Amazons, the mythical founders of the city, by Phidias, Polycletus, and other of the classic masters; there was Appelles' famous painting of Alexander wielding a thunderbolt, and from a constant stream of visitors and votaries came numberless contributions in money and objects of virtu. From lands and other sources the temple derived an enormous revenue, and here was also stored for safe-keeping much of the wealth of Asia, monarchs and subjects alike being glad to place their possessions under the guardianship of Diana of the Ephesians. Thus was this celebrated fane at once a sanctuary, a place of worship, a museum, and a bank, until in 262 it was plundered and destroyed by the Goths, together with the city itself. When Christianity supplanted the cult of Artemis, its remains were used as a quarry for the architectural embellishment, first of Constantinople, and then of Turkish mosques and Italian palaces. Later its site, covered deep with mud, remained for ages unknown, and was discovered only by an accident which in 1869 directed to the spot an explorer in the service of the British museum.

Smyrna, whose commerce had exalted it, twenty-six centuries ago, to a foremost rank among the Greek settlements of Asia Minor, is still the leading commercial emporium of the Levant. Though its origin is lost in the twilight of history, it has preserved an almost perfect continuity of record, at least from the days of its occupation by Ionian colonists. Still are to be seen the remains of the massive Ionic fortress which formed the landward

SULTAN OF TURKEY

defence of the town until its capture by the Lydians, where-after it sank into the condition of a village until restored and refortified on its present site by the successors of Alexander the Great, to whom, as is said, its rebuilding was suggested in a dream. As then it stood, it was a city of surpassing beauty, rising from the seaboard, tier above tier, on terraced hillside slopes toward the acropolis. Its streets were broad, well paved, and laid out in regular lines. There were several temples, and among its public buildings were a theatre, a stadium, and a gymnasium. With a present population of more than 200,000, Smyrna is now the chief port of Asiatic Turkey, and the terminus of a railway system which is being gradually extended into the most fertile valleys of Anatolia.

Trebizond, the Trapezus of the Greeks, was first made known to the western world after the retreat of the Ten Thousand, who rested there for a time from their long and toilsome journey from Cunaxa. After the dismemberment of the Byzantine empire it became, under the rule of the Commeni, a place of considerable note, its palace being famed for its splendor and its court for luxury, intrigue, and immorality. It was also a seat of learning and a resort for learned men, who furnished the palace library with valuable manuscripts, while skilful architects adorned the city with costly and elaborate buildings; the writers of the age, among them Cardinal Bessarion, describing in glowing terms its churches and monasteries, its stately towers, and its suburban groves and orchards. The largest of existing churches is that of the Virgin of the Golden Head, a plain but massive edifice now converted into a mosque. A more tasteful structure is the church of Haghia Sophia, with its handsome portico and lofty campanile, whose walls are decorated with frescos descriptive of religious themes. A few leagues from the town is the monastery of Sumelas, founded some fifteen centuries ago at the mouth of a cavern midway in a tall perpendicular cliff. It was rebuilt and richly endowed by Commenus III, whose golden bull is among its most valued relics.

In Turkish Armenia Erzeroum, its principal town, is still a place of some importance, though but a shadow of its former self, losing, it is said, at the time of its capture by the Seljuks, in 1201, more than thrice its present population. It is one of the most ancient of Armenian cities, and without exception the dirtiest, with narrow, tortuous streets, unpaved and badly drained, flanked by sombre buildings of dark-gray mud-cemented stone. There are many mosques and churches, of which the cathedral is the only one worthy of note as an architectural composition. As the chief emporium for the caravan trade between Persia and Black sea ports, Erzeroum has its full share of commerce, though sorely hampered by the unsettled condition of the people; for in Armenia Turks and Christians cannot dwell together in peace.

For the three centuries or more during which Cyprus has been in the hands of the Turks, its annals are almost a blank, except for occasional insurrections and massacres, its former prosperity giving place to stagnation and decay; so that the largest town, Lucarna, on the site of ancient Citium, has but 6,000 or 7,000 inhabitants. Though of its antiquities little is known, there have been unearthed many statues and other works showing a strange intermixture of Hellenic and Oriental art. In Crete, or Candia, recent explorations have added much to our knowledge of this ancient land, famed as the birthplace of Olympian deities, as the site of the Minos legend, and as the seat of a civilization so ancient that Lycurgus, it is said, borrowed its laws and institutions. Rhodes, under whose Colossus passed the triremes of the Greeks, has now several lines of steamers calling at its port; for commerce is increasing rapidly, and especially the transit trade. Of this gigantic monument, laid prostrate by earthquake in 224 B.C., after keeping guard over the harbor for more than half a century, its enormous fragments were the wonder of the world until after the island was conquered by the Saracens, when the remains were sold for their worth as old metal, and loaded on the backs of 900 camels. As Strabo relates, Rhodes surpassed all other cities in beauty of design and decorative features, containing 3,000 statues, among which were many of exceptional merit, together with paintings by Protogenes and other masters, It was a city of arts and arms, the mistress of the sea, and with vast accumulations of wealth, until, for embracing the cause of Caesar, it was plundered by Cassius, and later reduced to a Ionian province.

MISCELLANY. — The foreign indebtedness of Turkey amounted in 1894 to about $660,000,000, in addition to which a war indemnity of $160,000,000 is being paid to Russia in installments of $1,600,000 a year. Taxation is oppressive, chiefly on account of its unequal distribution, and especially for the tithes demanded on agricultural products. In the army, including the militia, more than 700,000 men are available as combatants, and in the navy there are over 100 vessels, most of them of obsolete pattern.

During a visit to Europe the sultan was so greatly impressed with the advantages of railway communication that he at once planned a system which would open up his empire and bring Constantinople into connection with European lines. Concessions, guarantees, and privileges were granted, $100,000,000 being subscribed merely as a beginning, while the various projects included also Asiatic Turkey; so that the visitor might travel almost entirely by rail from London or Paris to the site of Troy or the ruins of the temple of Diana of the Ephesians.

The earthquakes of earlier centuries and the conflagrations of modern times have left but few relics of the former capital of the Byzantian empire and of the earlier sultans. Around the hippodrome they are most numerous, including the remains of palaces, churches,

OBELISK OF
THEODOSIUS

and columns with which are associated the names of Constantine, Theodosius, Chrysostom, and others of historic renown. In the fire of 1870 more than 3,000 buildings were burned, and it is said that the losses by fire are equal to the entire destruction of the city once every twenty years.

COLOSSUS OF RHODES

The interior of Asia Minor is a vast table-land, nowhere less than 2,000 feet above the sea except for occasional valleys. It is traversed by many mountain ranges, rising to an elevation of 7,000 to 11,000 feet. Most of the rivers are small, and none are navigable for any considerable distance. The climate of the up-lands is dry and the temperature subject to great extremes, large tracts consisting of bare and treeless downs fit only for the pasturage of sheep. In more favored districts are vineyards, orchards, olive and walnut groves, and tobacco plantations, while cotton thrives near the sea-shore and silk is largely produced in the neighborhood of Broussa. What are known as Smyrna figs and raisins are mainly produced in the valley of the Maeander, and opium, madder, and saffron are among the agricultural products. Of domestic animals the camel and buffalo rank first in value; cattle and horses are few and of inferior breed; vast herds of sheep are depastured on the plains, and still in demand is the hair of the Angora goat, from which shawls are made little inferior to those of Kashmir. Minerals are plentiful, but little utilized. The silver and copper mines of the north, and the marble quarries, especially the Phrygian marbles so much in favor with the Romans, are now almost neglected. There are coal deposits near Heraclea, on the Black sea coast, and still the iron ores in the country of the Chalybes are worked in the same primitive fashion as in the days of the Greeks.

During the reign of Abdul Aziz the expenses of the court kitchens were over $2,500,000 a year.

A few centuries before the Christian era, Miletus, whose site near the mouth of the Maeander is now a morass, was by far the wealthiest and most powerful city in Asia Minor, founding itself more than threescore settlements, among which were Cyzicus, Abydus, and Sinope. Of its four harbors, one was spacious, and all were well protected; its Black sea trade was enormous, and its commerce extended along the entire coast of the Levant. After the revolt of 500 B.C., which followed the Persian conquest, its inhabitants were massacred or led into captivity by Darius, whereafter its annals are of no special interest. Miletus was a literary as well as a commercial centre, its philosophers including Thales and his successor Anaximander.

By the treaty of Berlin it is provided that the prince of Bulgaria shall be elected by the people, and their choice confirmed by the Sublime Porte with the consent of the European powers, no member of the royal families of Europe being eligible. The principality has an army mustering, inclusive of militia, nearly 200,000 men, and there are a few small vessels of war. Exports for 1894 amounted to nearly $20,000,000, with imports of about equal amount. The National bank of Bulgaria, with headquarters at Sona and several branches, has a capital of $2,000,000, furnished by the state, and in each district is an agricultural bank under government control.

PRINCE FERDINAND
OF BULGARIA

When Alcmaeon of Athens returned from the temple of Delphi, where he had assisted the royal messengers in presenting the gifts of Croesus, the monarch told him to go into his treasury and take thence what he would, whereupon, as the legend is, the Athenian filled the skirt of his tunic, his boots, and even his hair with gold-dust. Croesus laughed when he saw him so heavily laden that he could barely walk, and said to him, "All this you may have and as much more as you wish." With the gold-producing regions of Asia Minor the Delphic and other Greek temples maintained unbroken intercourse, entering into business relations with all the Hellenic colonies, and serving, as I have said, in place of banks.

Europe has standing armies aggregating from 3,000,000 to 4,000,000 men, which cost $1,000,000,000 or more to keep up, producers to pay the bills, and all for the pleasure of such rulers and demagogues as may take delight in seeing bands of men, having no quarrel and scarcely knowing what they are fighting for, meet and butcher each other. Add to this the cost of royalty, nobility, et cetera, with their vast progeny, and the creators of wealth have their hands full. The cost of heavy cannon, per ton, is for cast iron $100, Armstrong $500, Krupp $850, Whitworth $875. At Waterloo the English artillery fired 9,467 rounds, or one for every Frenchman killed.

RESURCES

Learn more about Hubert Howe Bancroft

In addition to The Book of Wealth, Hubert Howe Bancroft wrote and published dozens of books on the history and settlement of the American West, the 1893 World's Fair and more.

To learn more about Bancroft and his business enterprises, the creation of the Bancroft Library at the University of California, Berkeley, and Bancroft's many other publications, visit:

www.BancroftBookofWealth.com/resources

Made in the USA
Lexington, KY
15 September 2016